COUNTRY

ISBN 978-1-5400-3814-2

HAL•LEONARD®

For all works contained herein:
Unauthorized copying, arranging, adapting, recording, Internet posting, public performance,
or other distribution of the music in this publication is an infringement of copyright.
Infringers are liable under the law.

Visit Hal Leonard Online at
www.halleonard.com

Contact us:
Hal Leonard
7777 West Bluemound Road
Milwaukee, WI 53213
Email: info@halleonard.com

In Europe, contact:
Hal Leonard Europe Limited
42 Wigmore Street
Marylebone, London, W1U 2RN
Email: info@halleonardeurope.com

In Australia, contact:
Hal Leonard Australia Pty. Ltd.
4 Lentara Court
Cheltenham, Victoria, 3192 Australia
Email: info@halleonard.com.au

Achy Breaky Heart
(Don't Tell My Heart)

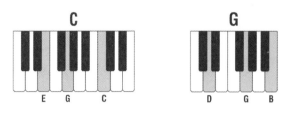

Words and Music by
Don Von Tress

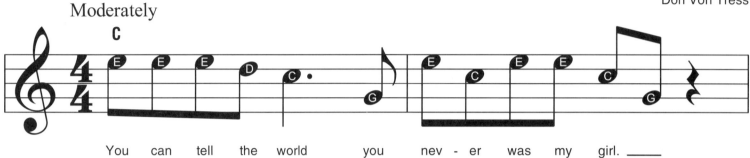

You can tell the world you nev - er was my girl. _____

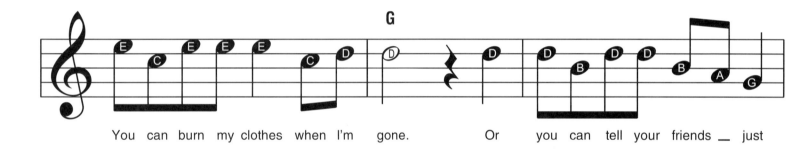

You can burn my clothes when I'm gone. Or you can tell your friends _ just

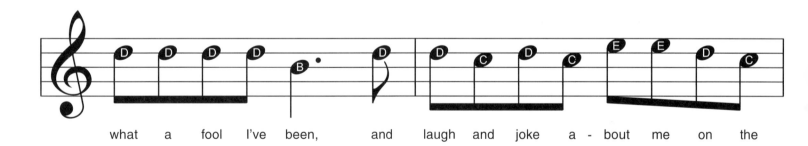

what a fool I've been, and laugh and joke a - bout me on the

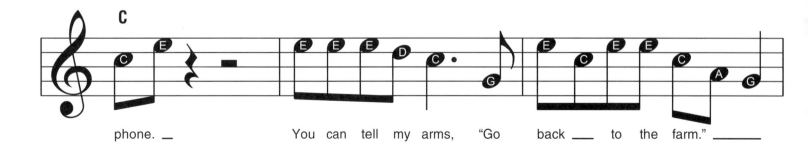

phone. _ You can tell my arms, "Go back _ to the farm." _____

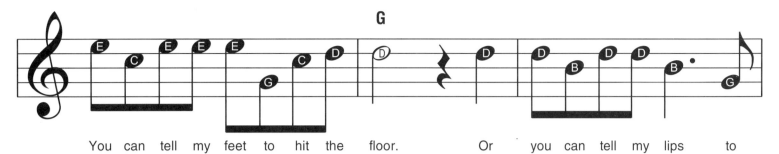

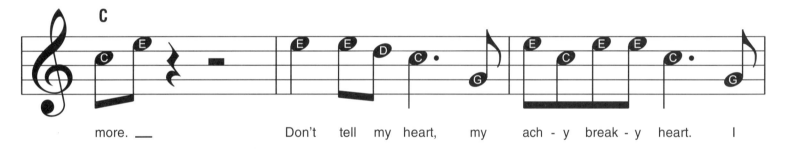

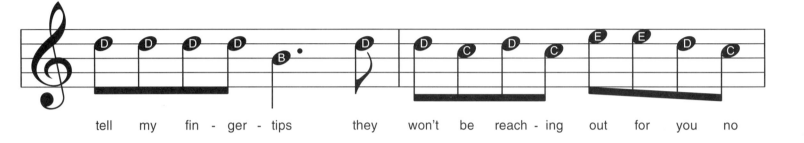

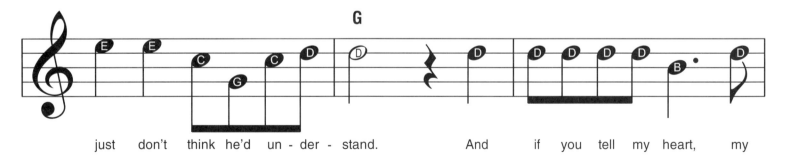

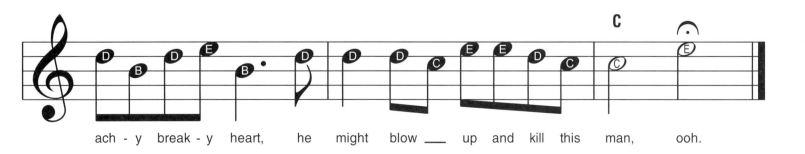

5

Always on My Mind

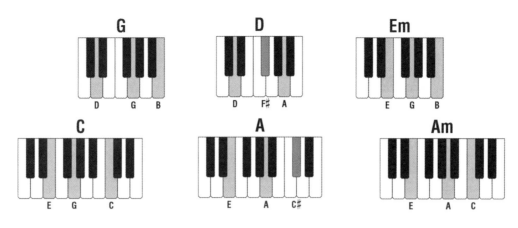

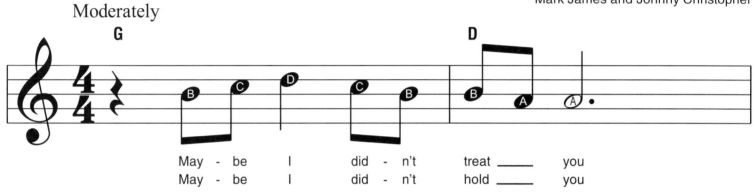

Words and Music by Wayne Thompson,
Mark James and Johnny Christopher

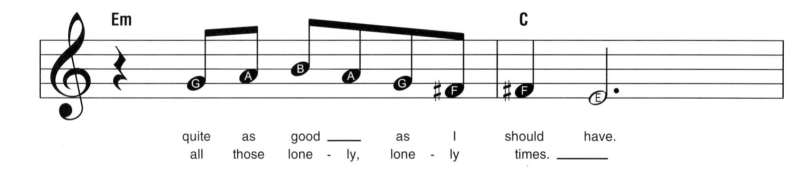

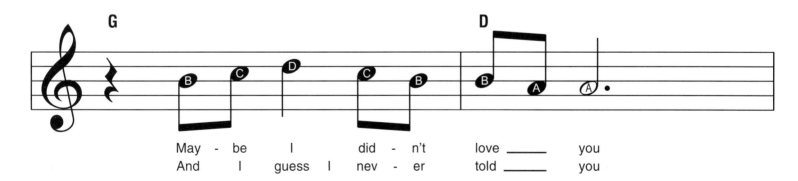

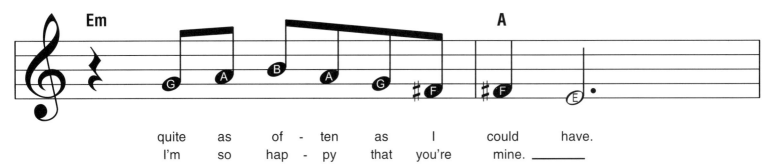

quite as of - ten as I could have.
I'm so hap - py that you're mine. _____

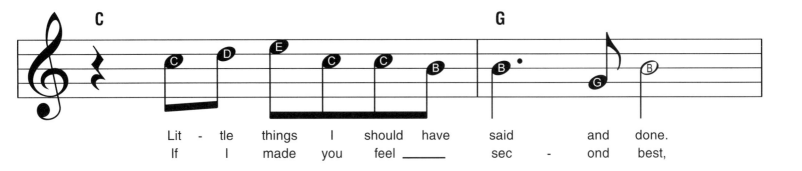

Lit - tle things I should have said and done.
If I made you feel _____ sec - ond best,

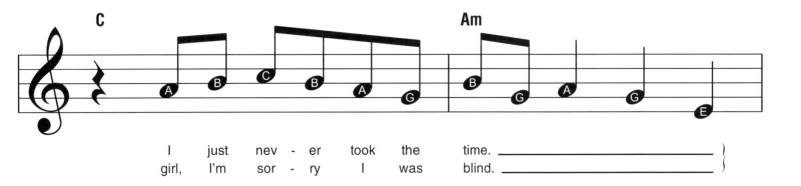

I just nev - er took the time. _____
girl, I'm sor - ry I was blind. _____

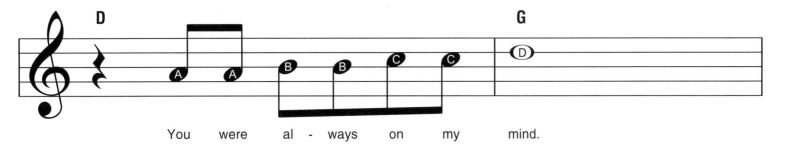

You were al - ways on my mind.

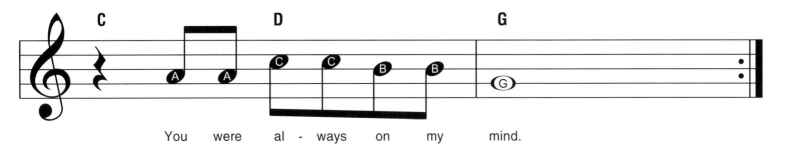

You were al - ways on my mind.

Amazed

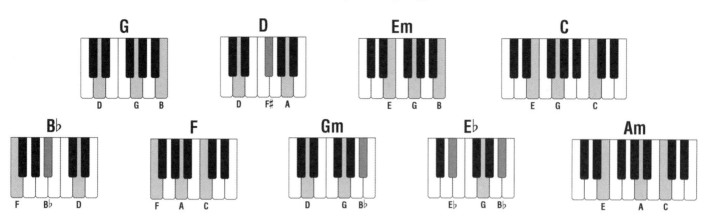

Words and Music by Marv Green,
Chris Lindsey and Aimee Mayo

Moderately

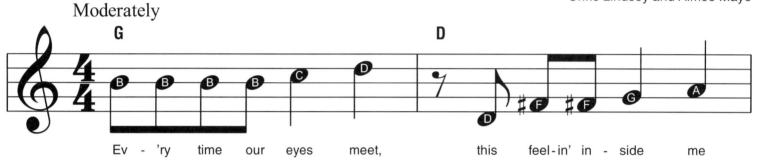

Ev - 'ry time our eyes meet, this feel-in' in - side me

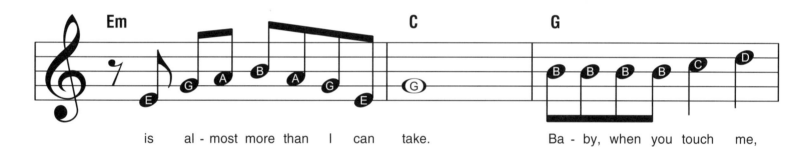

is al - most more than I can take. Ba - by, when you touch me,

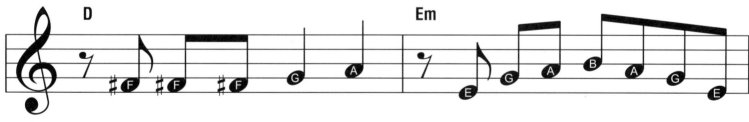

I can feel how much you love me, and it just blows me a -

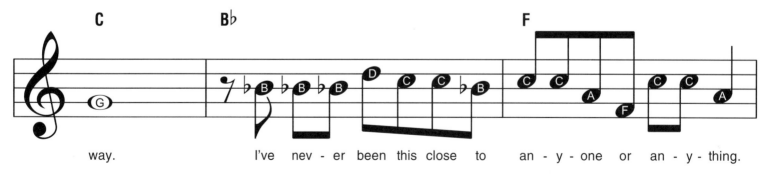

way. I've nev - er been this close to an - y - one or an - y - thing.

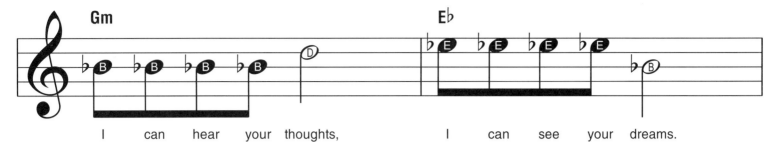

I can hear your thoughts, I can see your dreams.

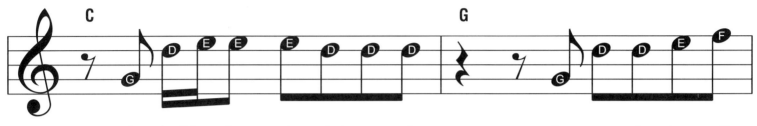

I don't know how you do what you do. I'm so in love with

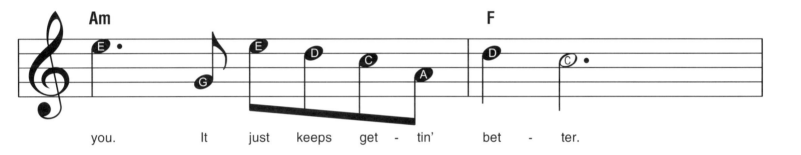

you. It just keeps get - tin' bet - ter.

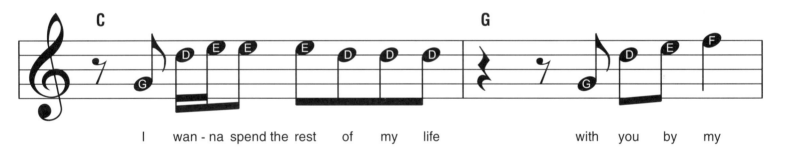

I wan - na spend the rest of my life with you by my

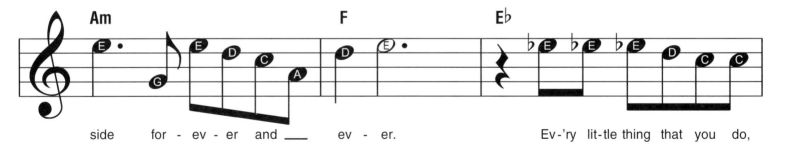

side for - ev - er and ___ ev - er. Ev -'ry lit-tle thing that you do,

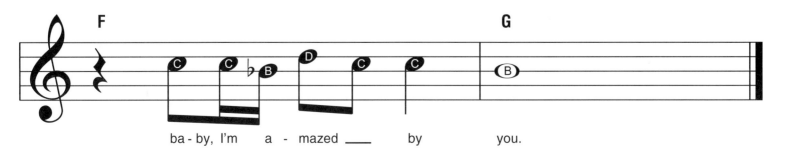

ba - by, I'm a - mazed ___ by you.

Blue Bayou

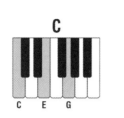
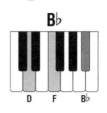
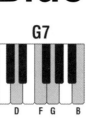
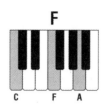

Words and Music by Roy Orbison
and Joe Melson

Moderately

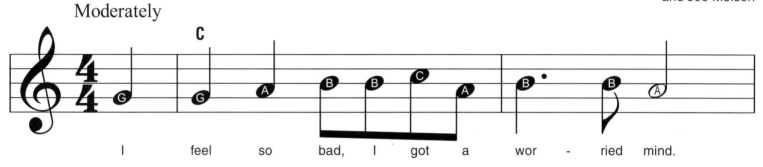

I feel so bad, I got a wor - ried mind.

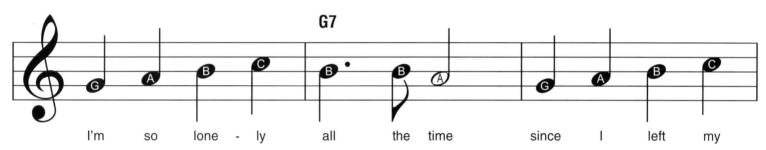

I'm so lone - ly all the time since I left my

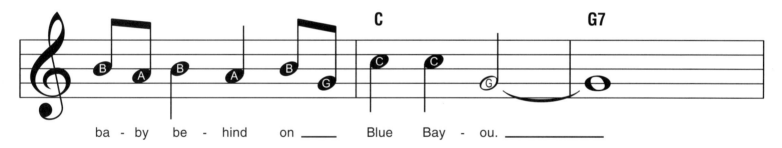

ba - by be - hind on ____ Blue Bay - ou. ____

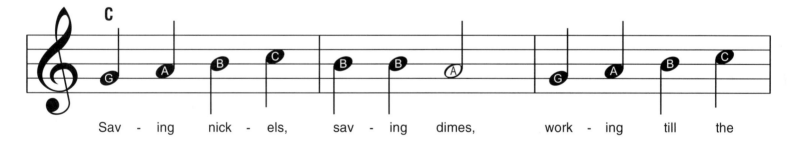

Sav - ing nick - els, sav - ing dimes, work - ing till the

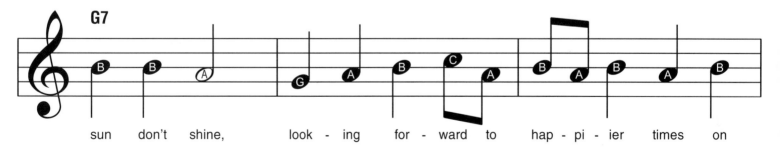

sun don't shine, look - ing for - ward to hap - pi - er times on

Blue Eyes Crying in the Rain

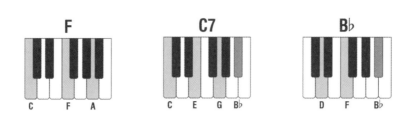

Words and Music by
Fred Rose

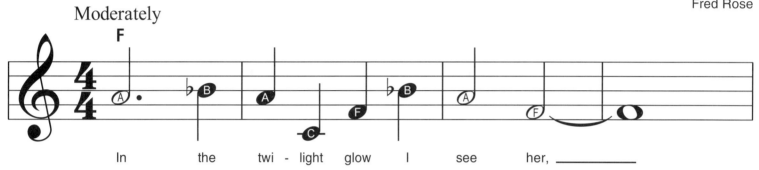

In the twi - light glow I see her, _____

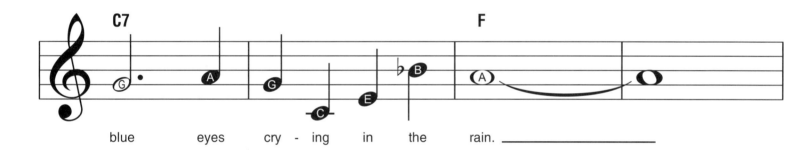

blue eyes cry - ing in the rain. _____

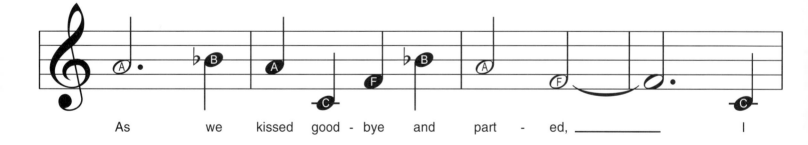

As we kissed good - bye and part - ed, _____ I

13

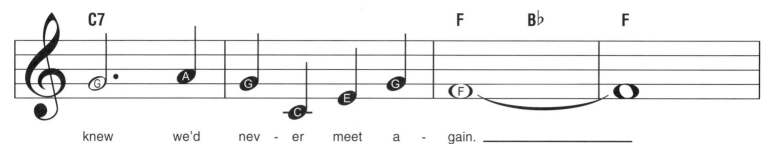

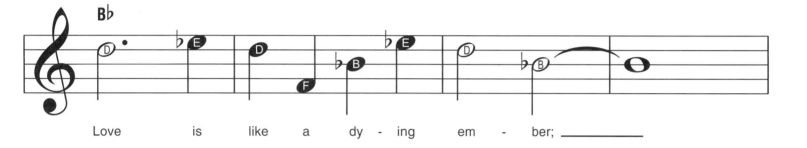

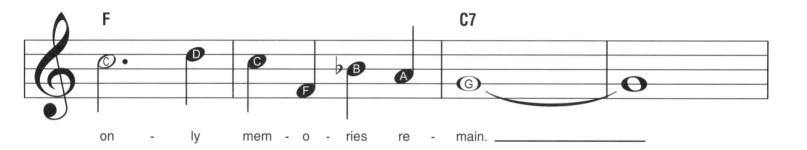

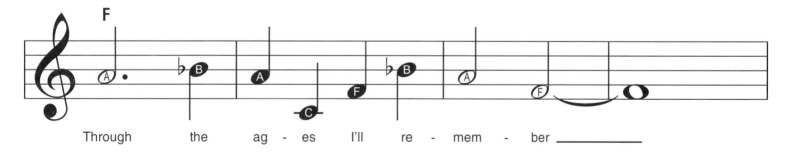

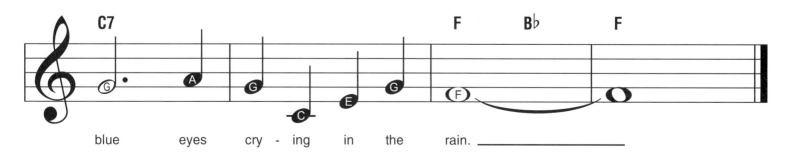

Chattahoochee

15

Coal Miner's Daughter

Words and Music by
Loretta Lynn

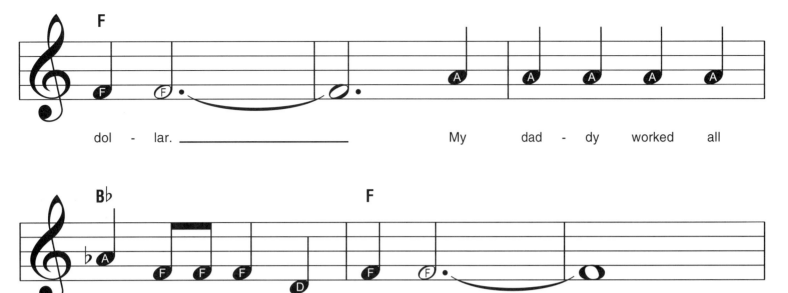

dol - lar. _____ My dad - dy worked all

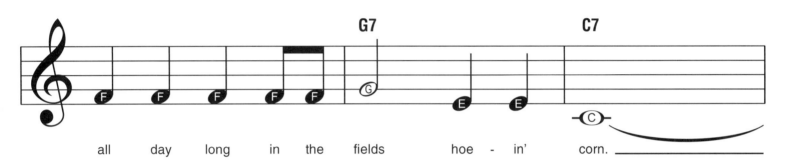

night in the Van Lear coal mine, _____

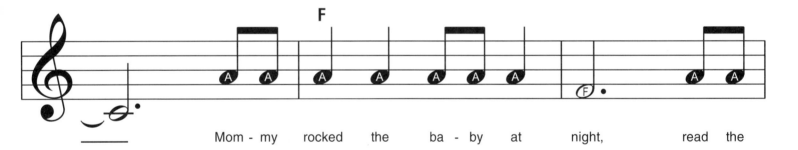

all day long in the fields hoe - in' corn. _____

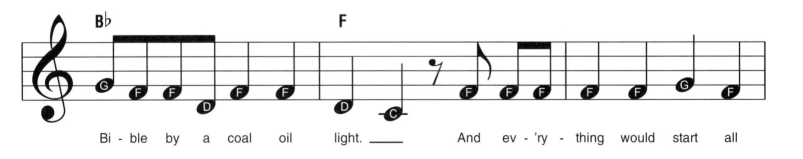

_____ Mom - my rocked the ba - by at night, read the

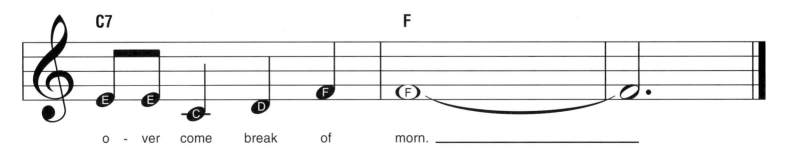

Bi - ble by a coal oil light. _____ And ev - 'ry - thing would start all

o - ver come break of morn. _____

Could I Have This Dance

from URBAN COWBOY

Words and Music by Wayland Holyfield
and Bob House

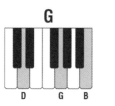
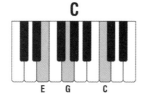
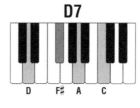
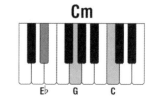

Moderate Waltz

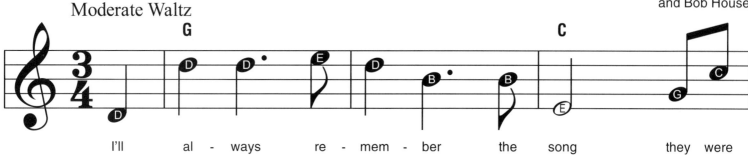

I'll al - ways re - mem - ber the song they were

play - ing the first time we danced and I knew. _____

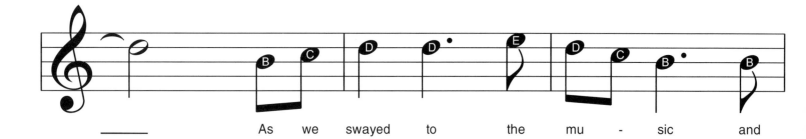

_____ As we swayed to the mu - sic and

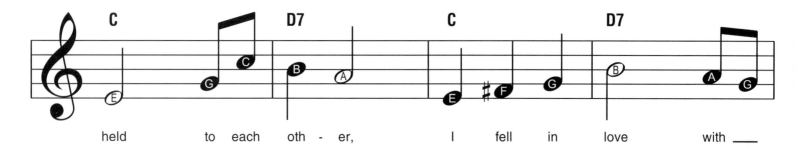

held to each oth - er, I fell in love with _____

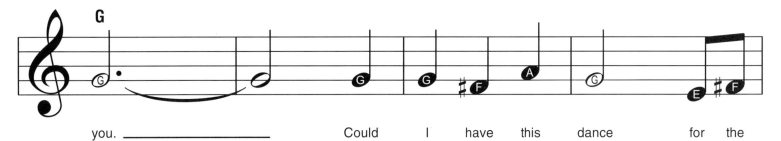

you. _____ Could I have this dance for the

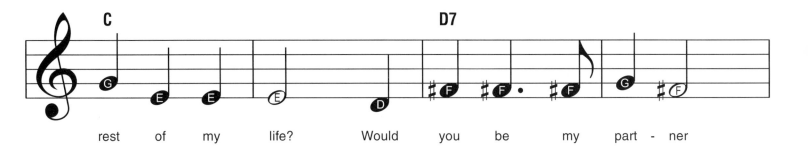

rest of my life? Would you be my part - ner

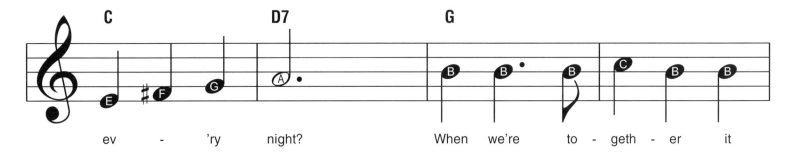

ev - 'ry night? When we're to - geth - er it

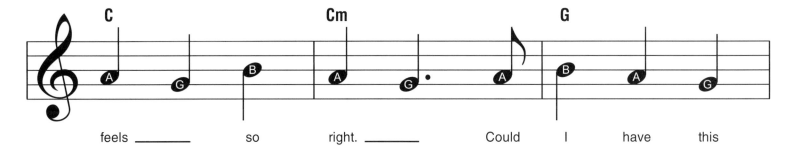

feels _____ so right. _____ Could I have this

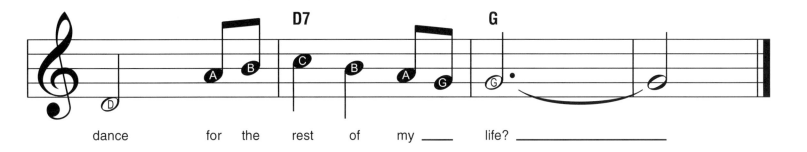

dance for the rest of my ____ life? _____

The Dance

Don't It Make My Brown Eyes Blue

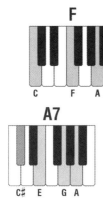
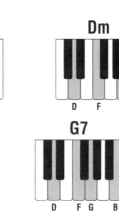
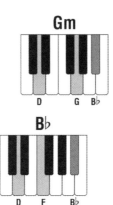
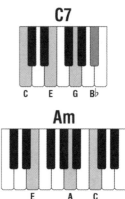

Words and Music by
Richard Leigh

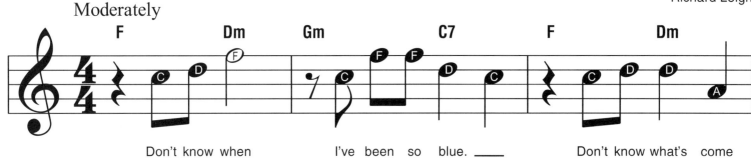

Don't know when   I've been so blue. ____   Don't know what's come

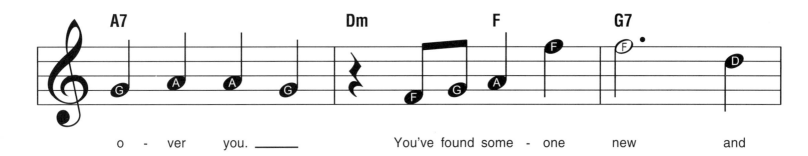

o - ver you. ____   You've found some - one   new   and

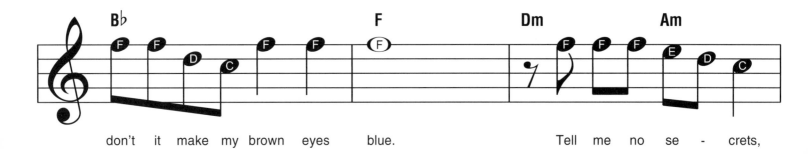

don't it make my brown eyes   blue.   Tell me no se - crets,

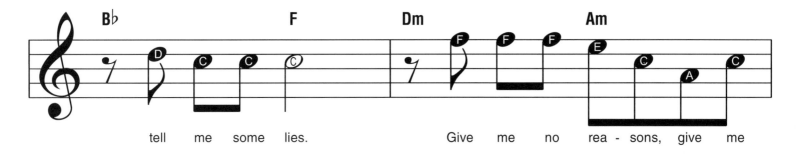

tell me some lies.   Give me no rea - sons, give me

El Paso

Words and Music by
Marty Robbins

Forever and Ever, Amen

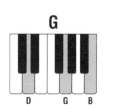
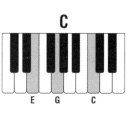
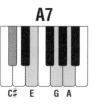
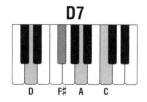

Words and Music by Paul Overstreet
and Don Schlitz

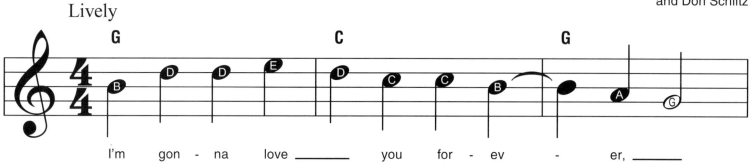

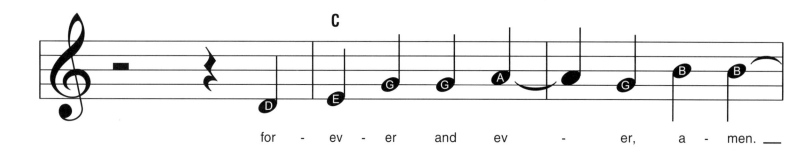

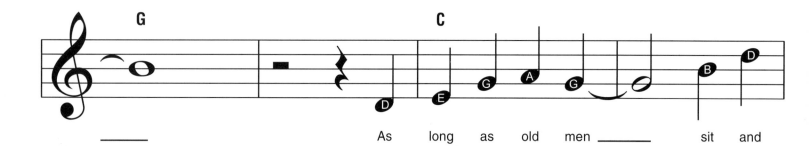

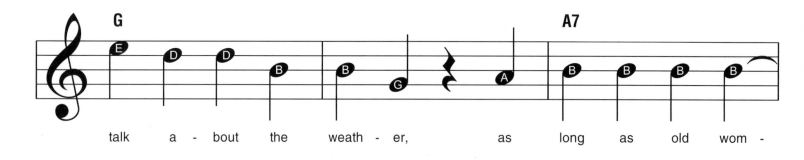

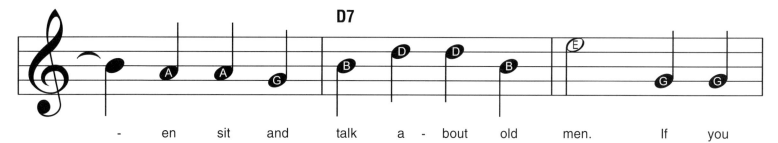

- en sit and talk a - bout old men. If you

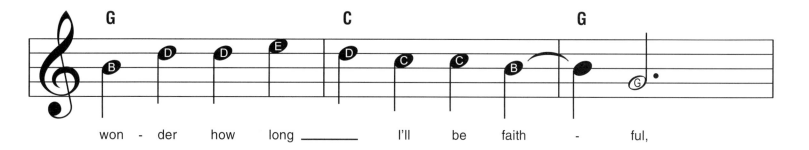

won - der how long _____ I'll be faith - ful,

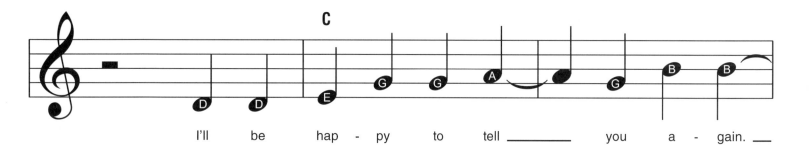

I'll be hap - py to tell _____ you a - gain. __

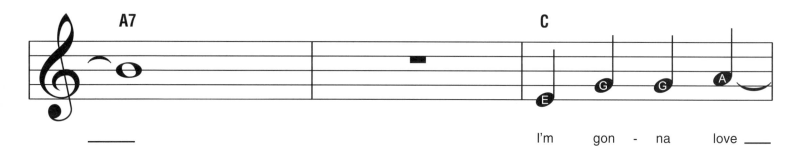

_____ I'm gon - na love ___

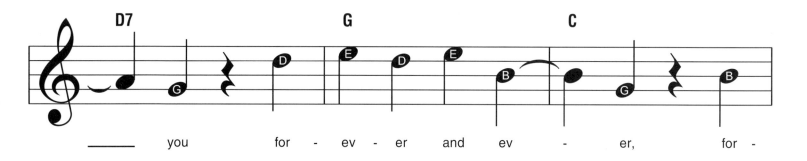

_____ you for - ev - er and ev - er, for -

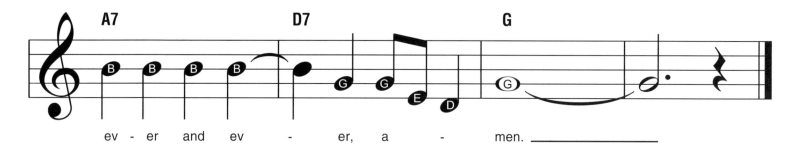

ev - er and ev - er, a - men. _____

Friends in Low Places

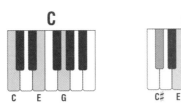

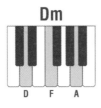
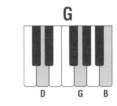

Words and Music by DeWayne Blackwell
and Earl Bud Lee

Moderately

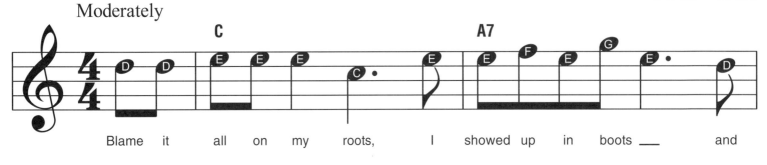

Blame it all on my roots, I showed up in boots ___ and

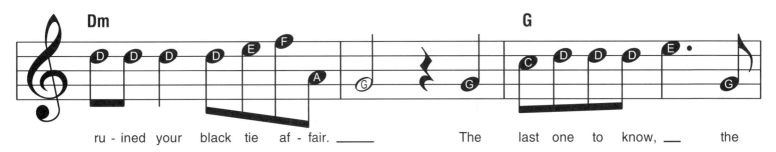

ru - ined your black tie af - fair. ____ The last one to know, ___ the

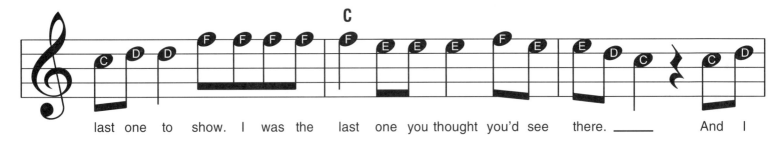

last one to show. I was the last one you thought you'd see there. ____ And I

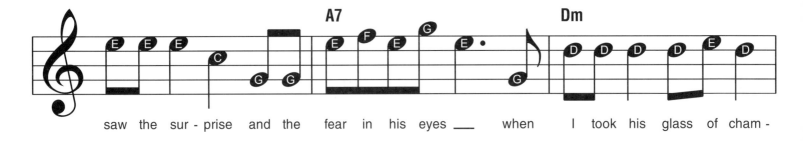

saw the sur - prise and the fear in his eyes ___ when I took his glass of cham -

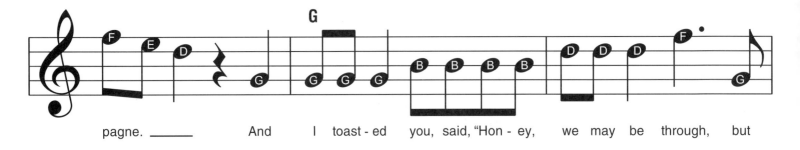

pagne. ____ And I toast - ed you, said, "Hon - ey, we may be through, but

Galveston

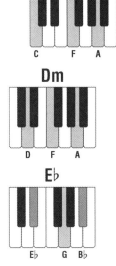
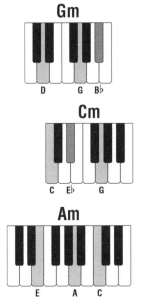
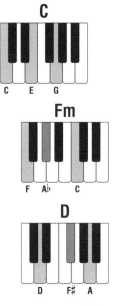
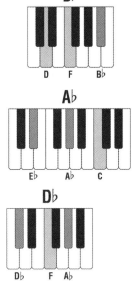

Words and Music by
Jimmy Webb

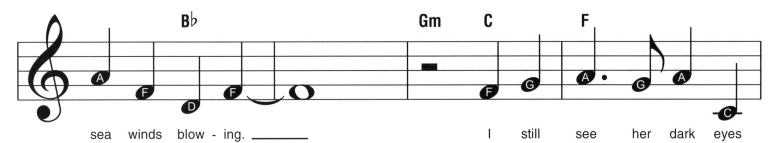

Gal - ves - ton, oh, Gal - ves - ton, _____ I still hear your

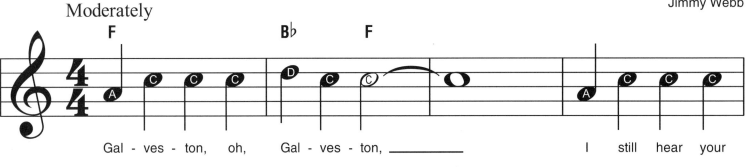

sea winds blow - ing. _____ I still see her dark eyes

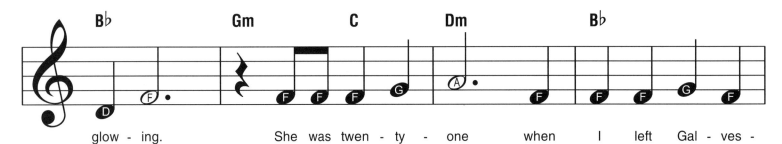

glow - ing. She was twen - ty - one when I left Gal - ves -

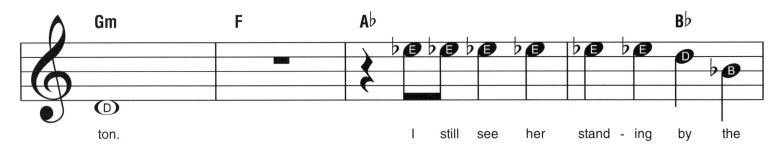

ton. I still see her stand - ing by the

The Gambler

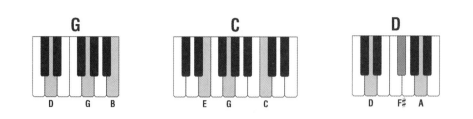

Words and Music by
Don Schlitz

On a warm sum-mer's eve-nin' on a train bound for
"Son, I've made a life out of read-in' peo-ple's

no-where, I met up with the gam-bler. We were both too tired to
fac-es and know-in' what their cards were by the way they held their

sleep. So we took turns a-star-in' out the win-dow at the
eyes. And if you don't mind my say-in', I can see you're out of

dark-ness 'til bore-dom o-ver-took us and he be-gan to
ac-es. For a taste of your

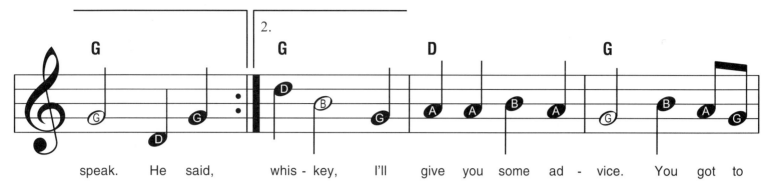

speak.   He said,   whis - key,   I'll   give   you   some   ad - vice.   You   got   to

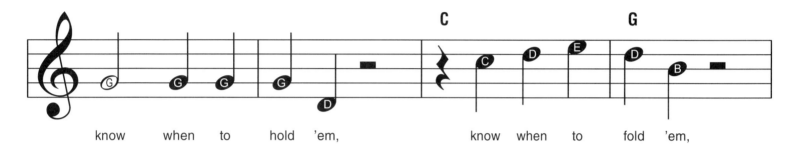

know   when   to   hold 'em,   know   when   to   fold 'em,

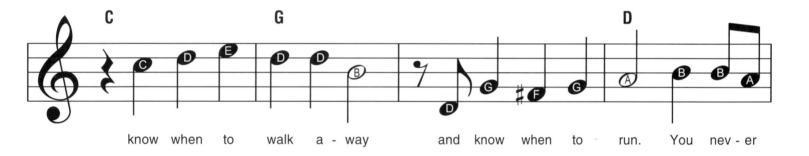

know   when   to   walk a - way   and   know   when   to   run.   You   nev - er

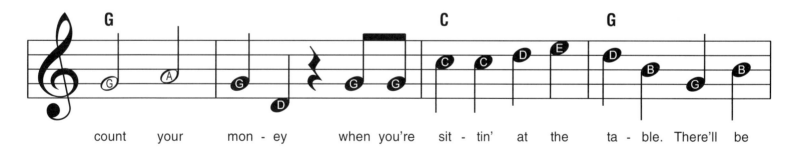

count   your   mon - ey   when you're   sit - tin'   at   the   ta - ble.   There'll   be

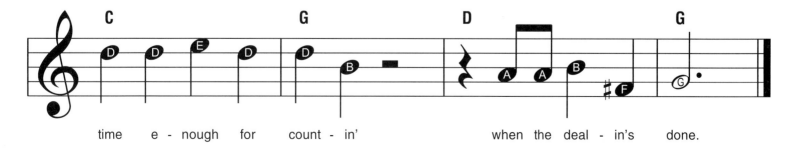

time   e - nough   for   count - in'   when   the   deal - in's   done.

Gentle on My Mind

Words and Music by
John Hartford

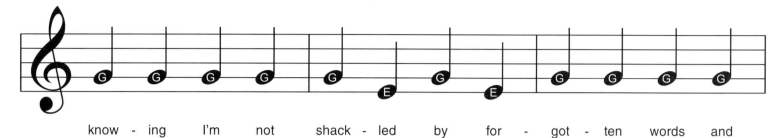

know - ing   I'm   not   shack - led   by   for - got - ten   words   and

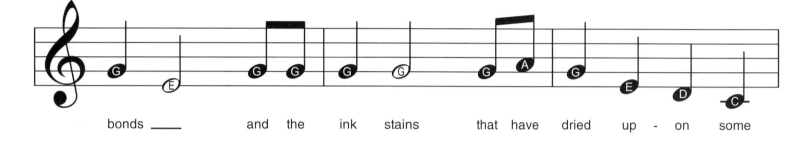

bonds _____   and   the   ink   stains   that   have   dried   up - on   some

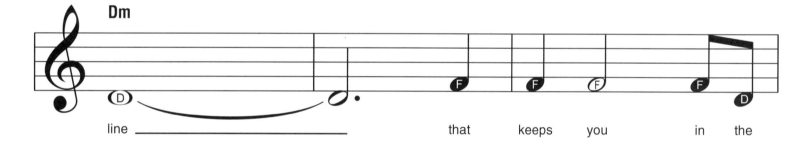

Dm

line _____   that   keeps   you   in   the

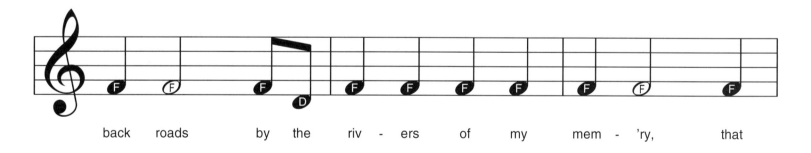

back   roads   by   the   riv - ers   of   my   mem - 'ry,   that

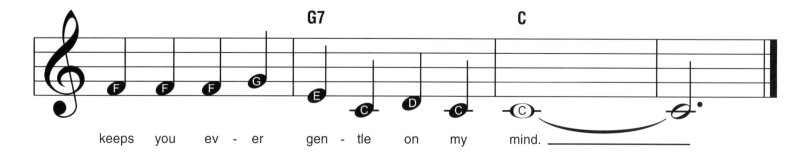

G7   C

keeps   you   ev - er   gen - tle   on   my   mind. _____

God Bless the U.S.A.

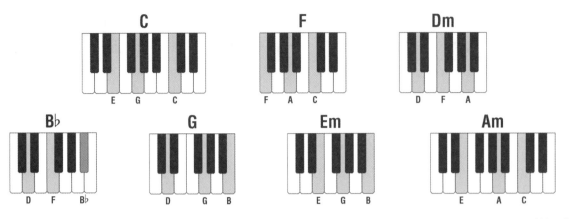

Words and Music by
Lee Greenwood

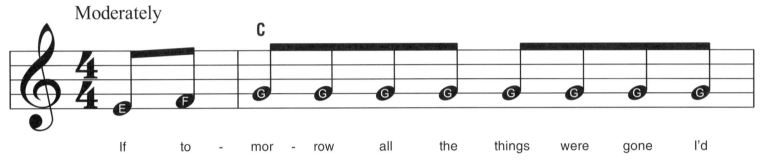

If to - mor - row all the things were gone I'd

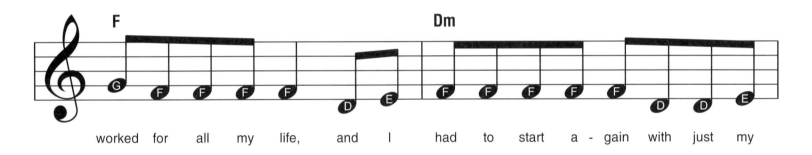

worked for all my life, and I had to start a - gain with just my

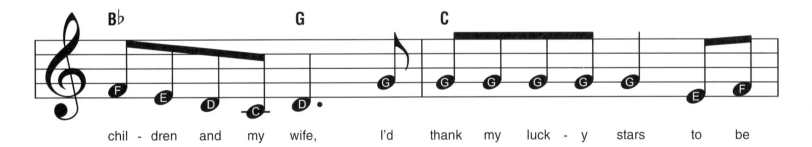

chil - dren and my wife, I'd thank my luck - y stars to be

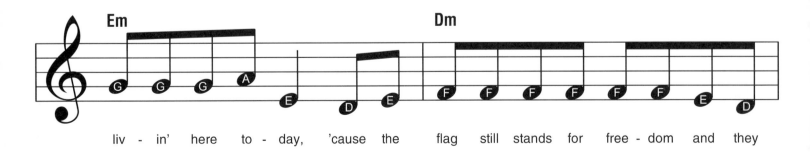

liv - in' here to - day, 'cause the flag still stands for free - dom and they

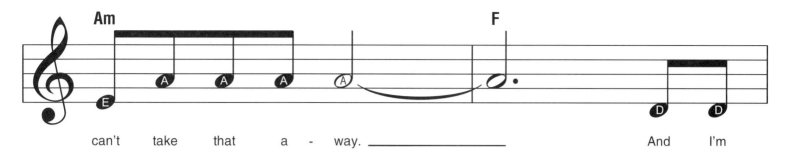

can't take that a - way. _____ And I'm

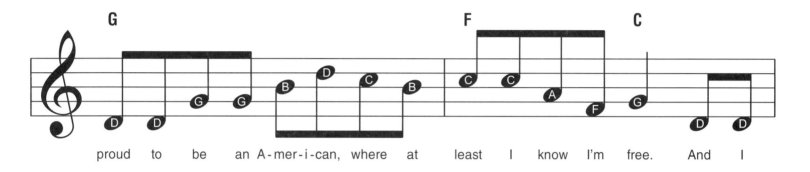

proud to be an A - mer - i -can, where at least I know I'm free. And I

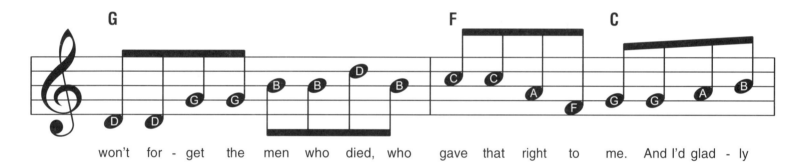

won't for - get the men who died, who gave that right to me. And I'd glad - ly

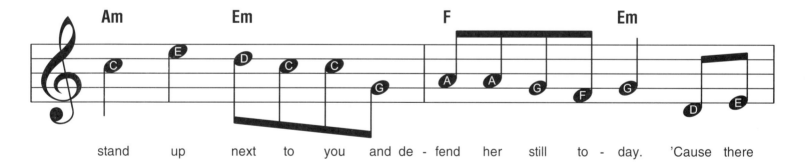

stand up next to you and de - fend her still to - day. 'Cause there

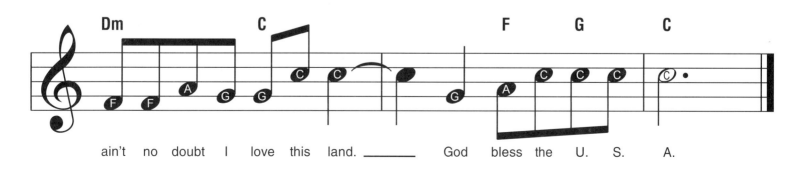

ain't no doubt I love this land. _____ God bless the U. S. A.

A Good Hearted Woman

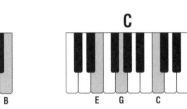
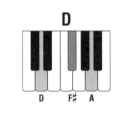

Words and Music by Willie Nelson
and Waylon Jennings

I Can't Stop Loving You

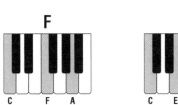 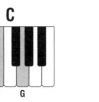 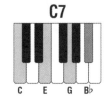

Words and Music by
Don Gibson

Green Green Grass of Home

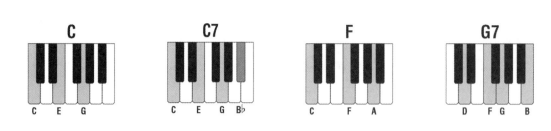

Words and Music by
Curly Putman

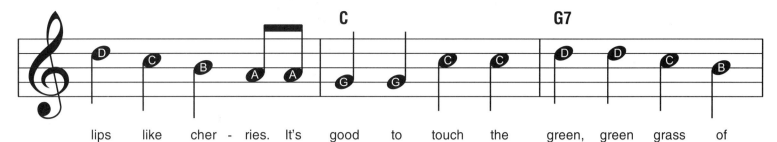

lips like cher - ries. It's good to touch the green, green grass of

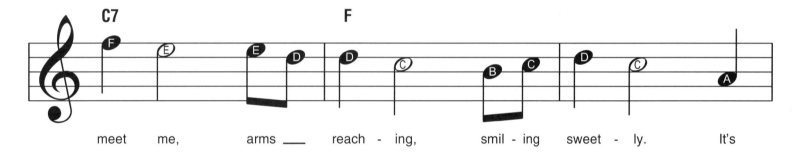

home. Yes, they'll all come to

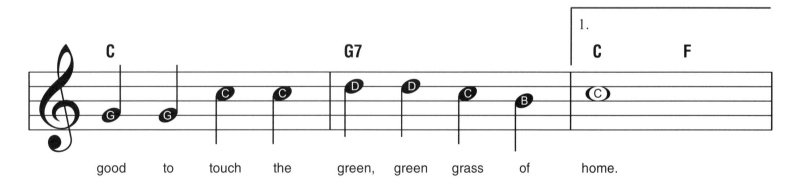

meet me, arms ___ reach - ing, smil - ing sweet - ly. It's

good to touch the green, green grass of home.

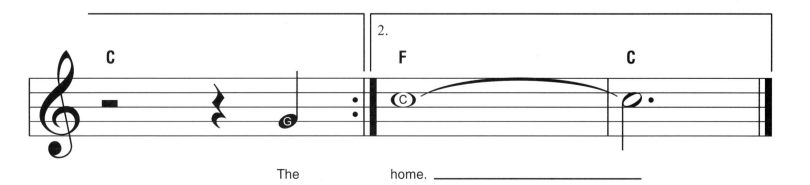

The home. _____

Happy Trails
from the Television Series THE ROY ROGERS SHOW

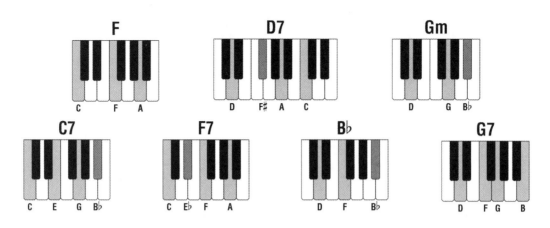

Words and Music by
Dale Evans

Moderately

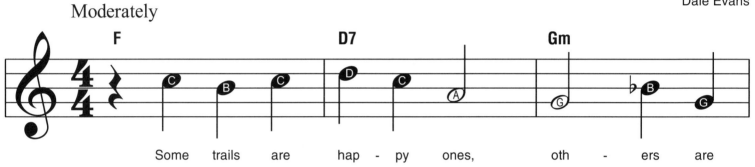

Some trails are hap - py ones, oth - ers are

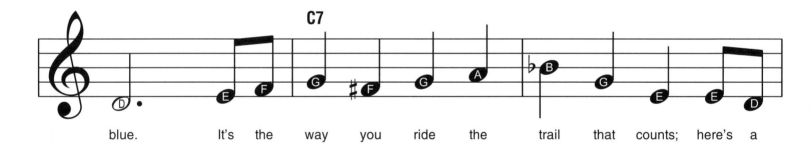

blue. It's the way you ride the trail that counts; here's a

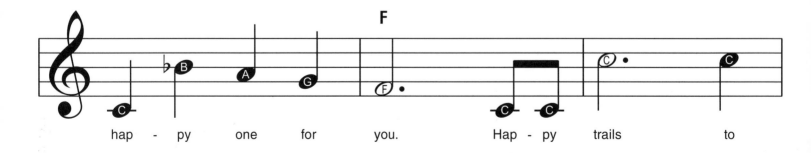

hap - py one for you. Hap - py trails to

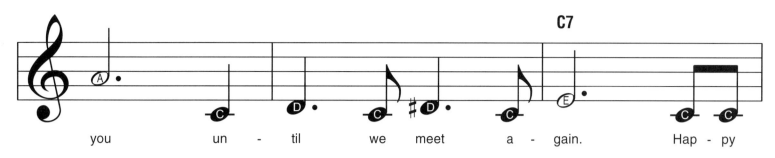

you un - til we meet a - gain. Hap - py

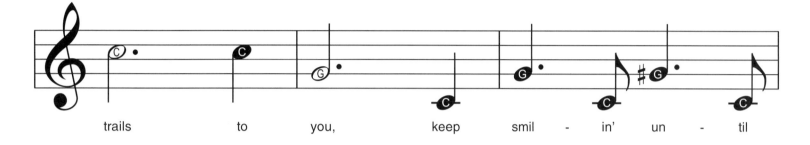

trails to you, keep smil - in' un - til

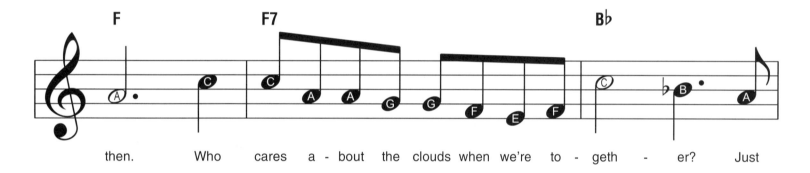

then. Who cares a - bout the clouds when we're to - geth - er? Just

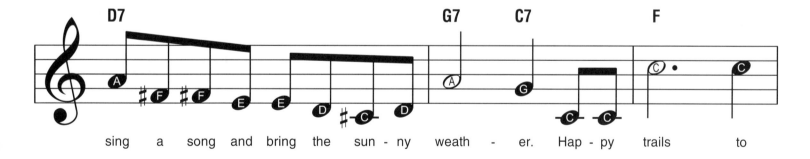

sing a song and bring the sun - ny weath - er. Hap - py trails to

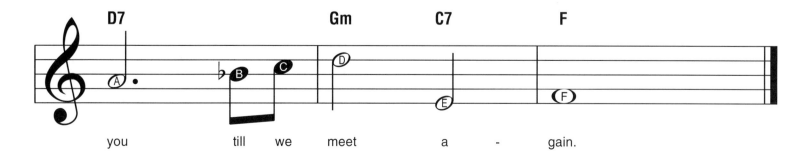

you till we meet a - gain.

He Stopped Loving Her Today

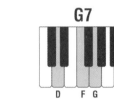

Words and Music by Bobby Braddock
and Curly Putman

Heartaches by the Number

Words and Music by
Harlan Howard

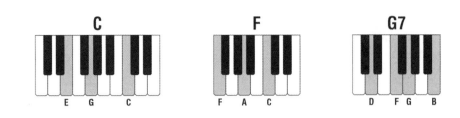

Heart - ache num - ber one was when you left me. _____ I

nev - er knew that I could hurt this way. _____ And

heart - ache num - ber two was when you came back a - gain.

You came back and nev - er meant to stay. Now I've got

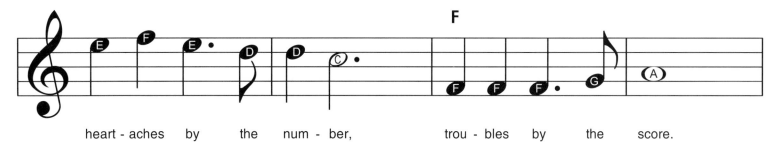

heart - aches by the num - ber, trou - bles by the score.

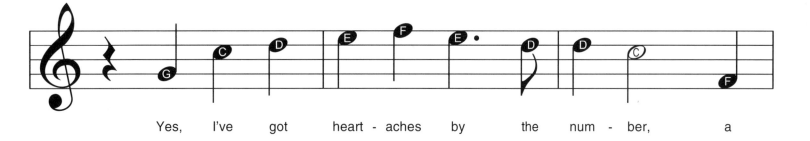

Ev - 'ry day you love me less, each day I love you more.

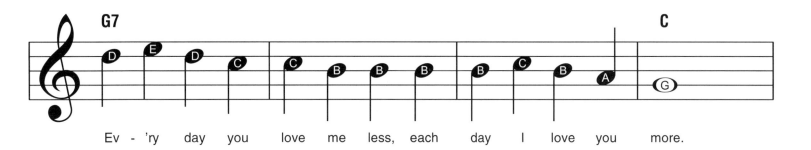

Yes, I've got heart - aches by the num - ber, a

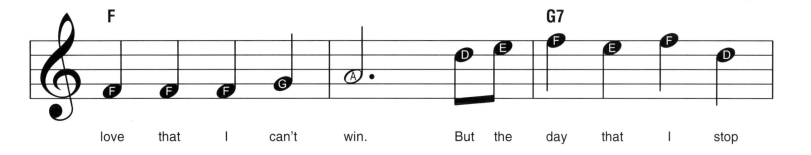

love that I can't win. But the day that I stop

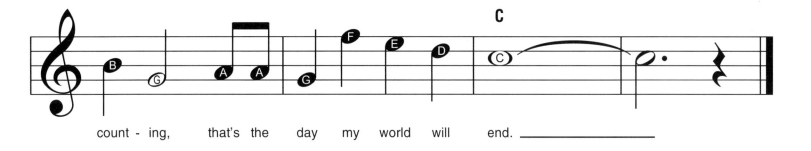

count - ing, that's the day my world will end. _____

Hello Darlin'

Words and Music by
Conway Twitty

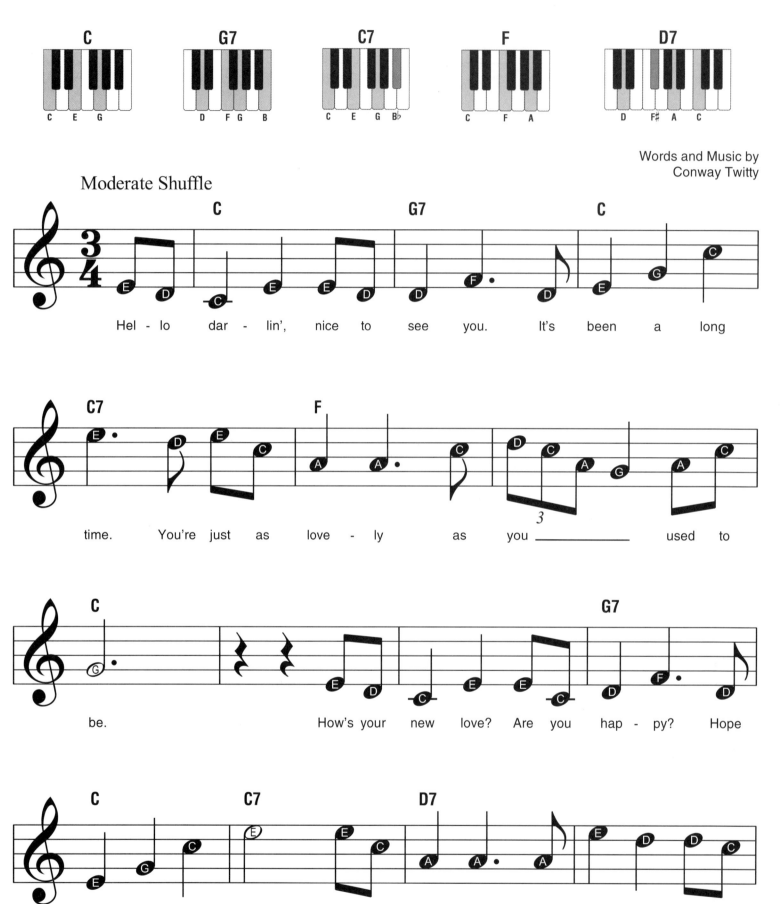

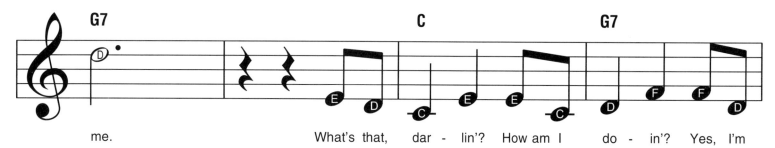

me.   What's that, dar - lin'? How am I   do - in'? Yes, I'm

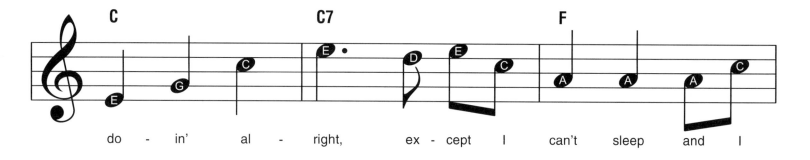

do - in' al - right, ex - cept I can't sleep and I

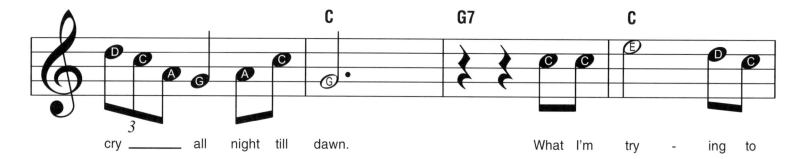

cry _____ all night till dawn.   What I'm try - ing to

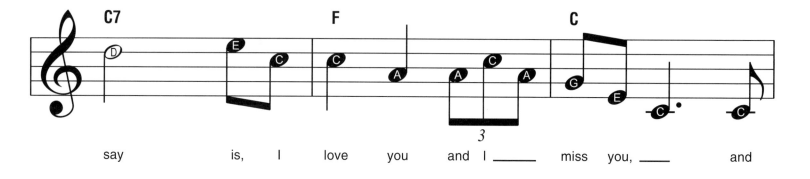

say   is, I love you and I _____ miss you, _____ and

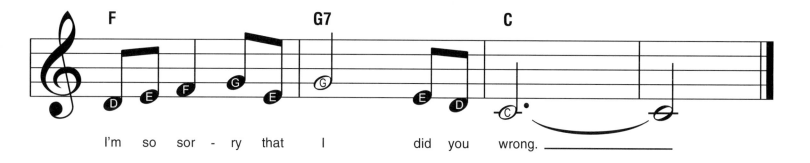

I'm so sor - ry that I did you wrong. _____

Here You Come Again

Words by Cynthia Weil
Music by Barry Mann

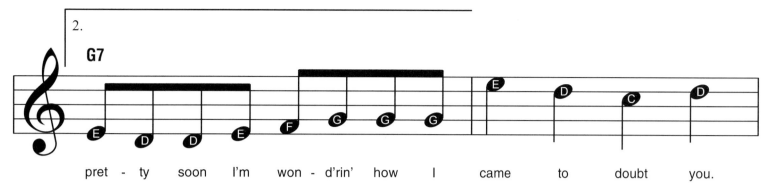

pret - ty soon I'm won - d'rin' how I came to doubt you.

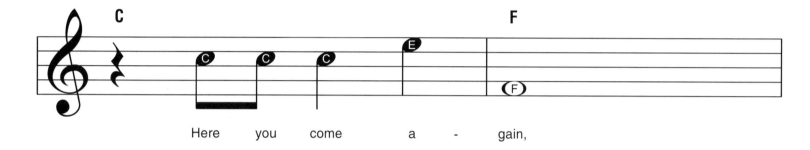

Here you come a - gain,

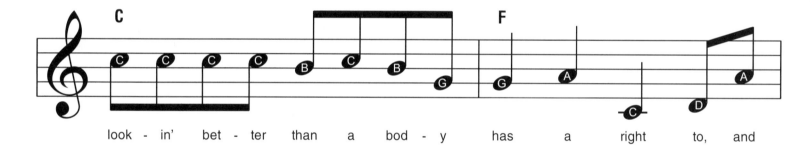

look - in' bet - ter than a bod - y has a right to, and

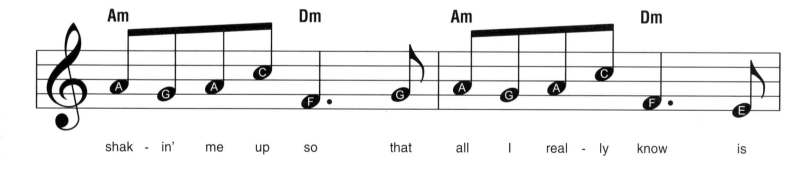

shak - in' me up so that all I real - ly know is

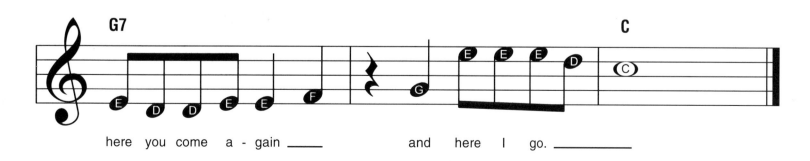

here you come a - gain _____ and here I go. _____

Hey, Good Lookin'

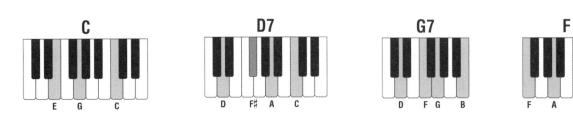

Words and Music by
Hank Williams

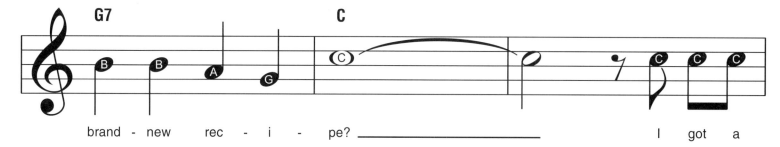

brand - new rec - i - pe? _____ I got a

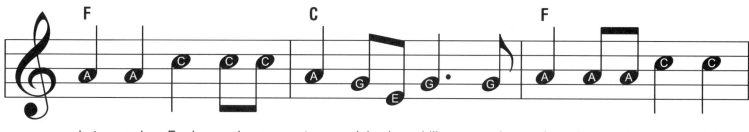

hot - rod Ford and a two - dol - lar bill, and I know a spot right

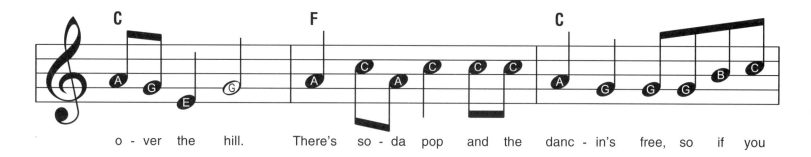

o - ver the hill. There's so - da pop and the danc - in's free, so if you

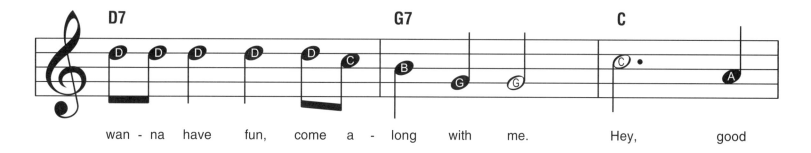

wan - na have fun, come a - long with me. Hey, good

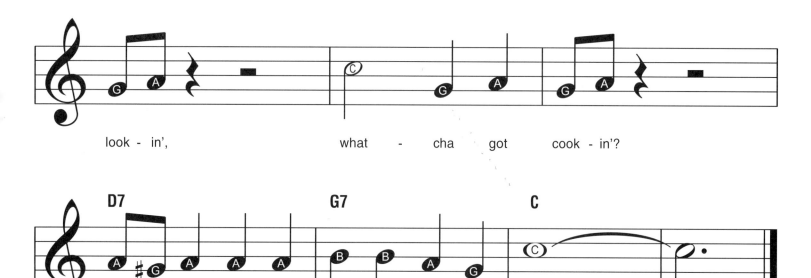

look - in', what - cha got cook - in'?

How's a - bout cook - in' some - thin' up with me? _____

I Love a Rainy Night

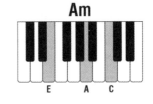

Words and Music by Eddie Rabbitt,
Even Stevens and David Malloy

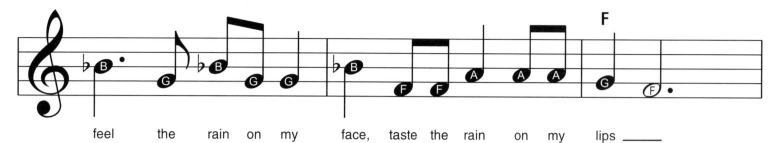

feel   the   rain   on   my   face,   taste   the   rain   on   my   lips _____

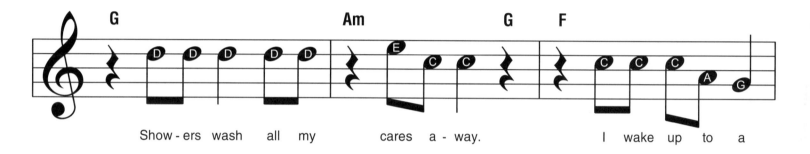

in   the   moon - light   shad - ows.

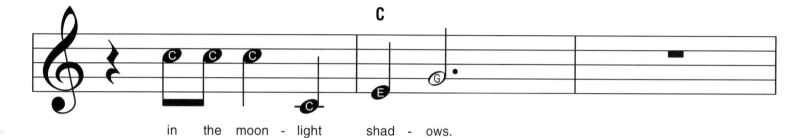

Show - ers   wash   all   my   cares   a - way.   I   wake   up   to   a

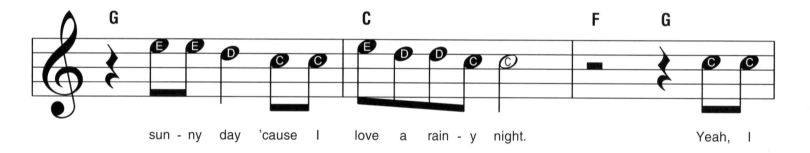

sun - ny   day   'cause   I   love   a   rain - y   night.   Yeah,   I

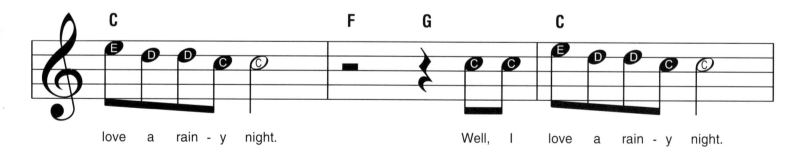

love   a   rain - y   night.   Well,   I   love   a   rain - y   night.

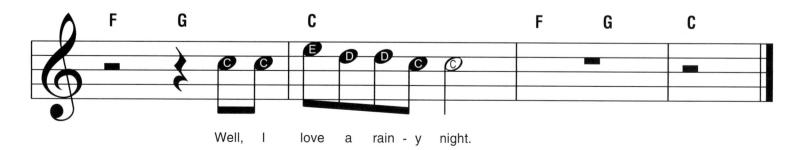

Well,   I   love   a   rain - y   night.

I Saw the Light

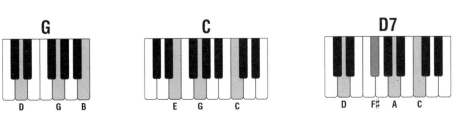

Words and Music by
Hank Williams

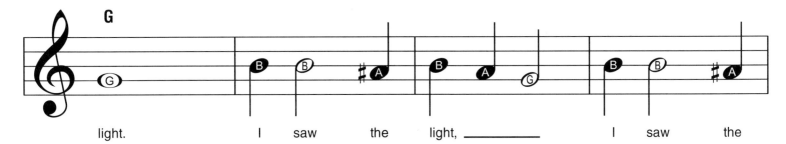

light.   I   saw   the   light, _____   I   saw   the

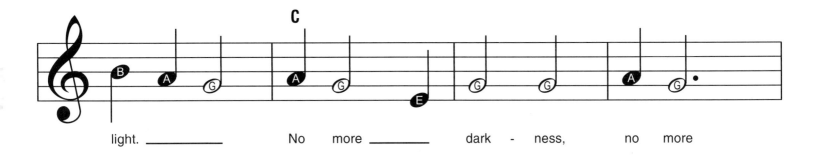

light. _____   No   more _____   dark - ness,   no   more

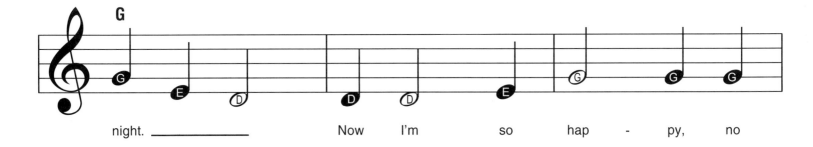

night. _____   Now   I'm   so   hap - py,   no

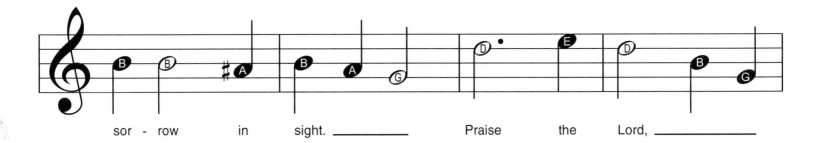

sor - row   in   sight. _____   Praise   the   Lord, _____

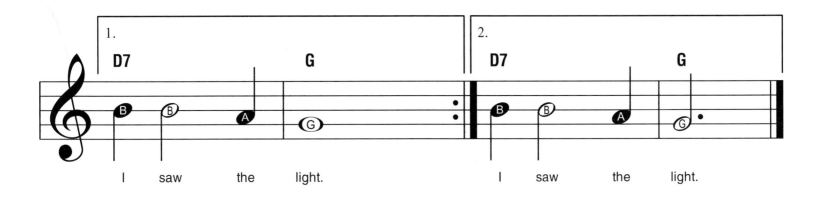

1.   I   saw   the   light.   2.   I   saw   the   light.

I Swear

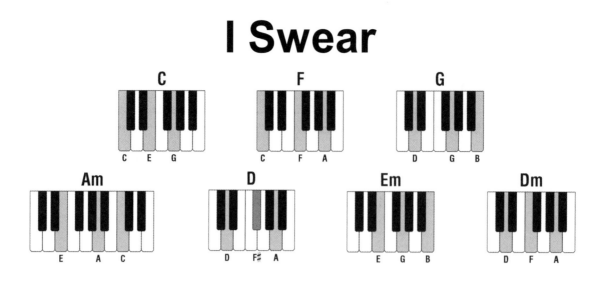

Words and Music by Frank Myers
and Gary Baker

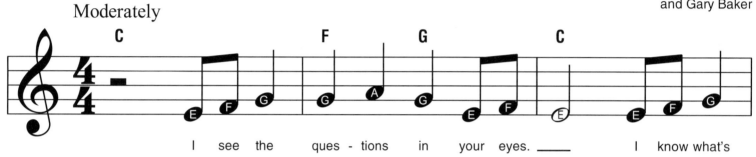

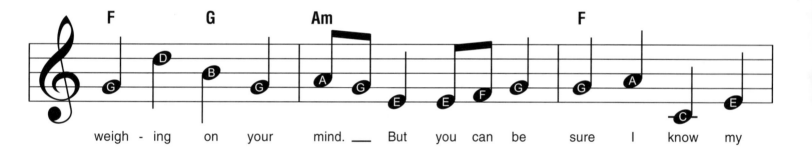

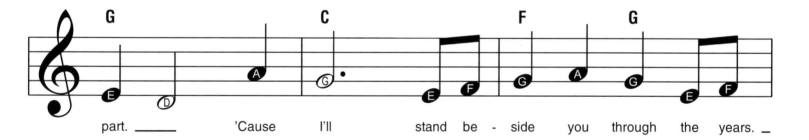

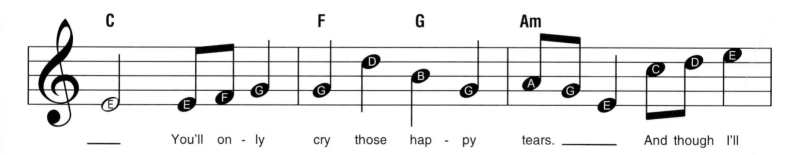

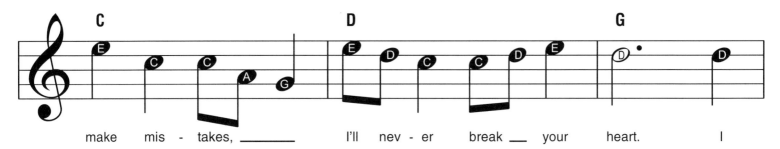

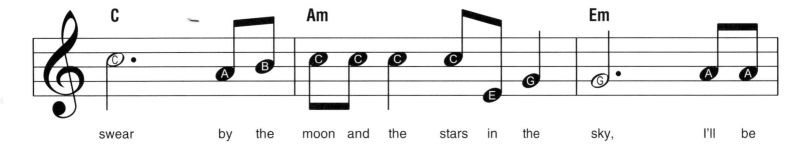

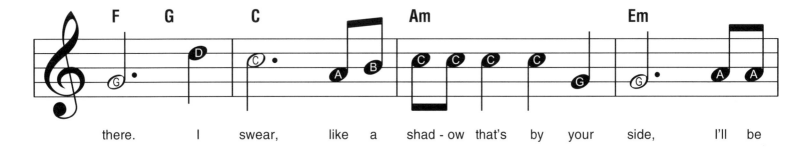

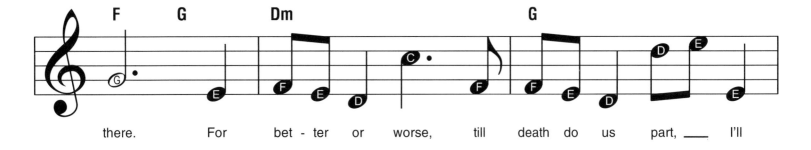

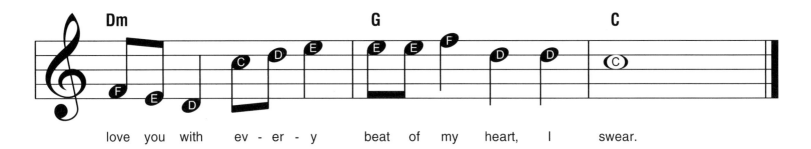

I Will Always Love You

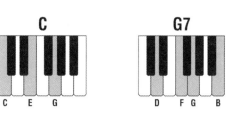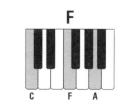

Words and Music by
Dolly Parton

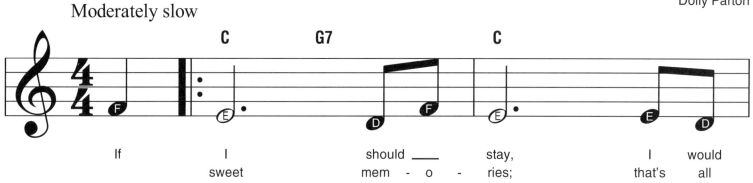

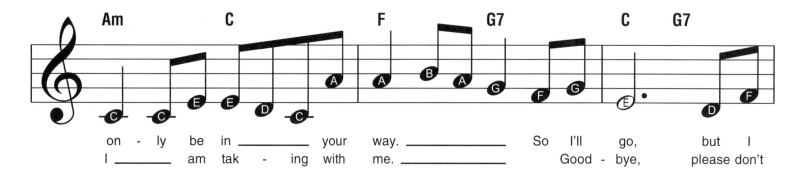

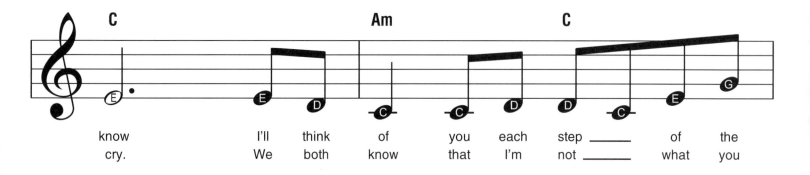

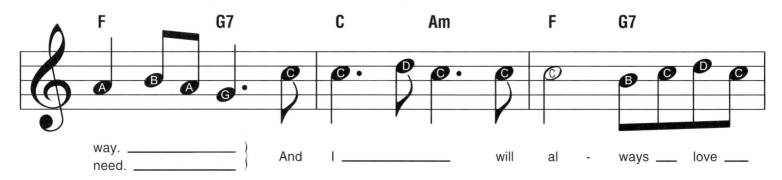

way. _____ ⎱
need. _____ ⎰ And I _____ will al - ways ___ love ___

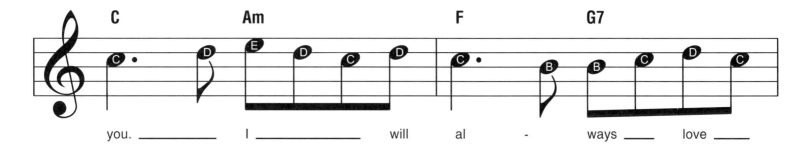

you. _____ I _____ will al - ways ___ love _____

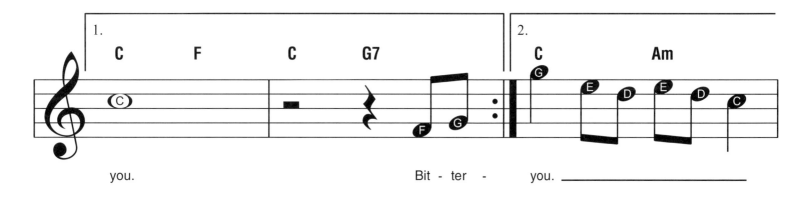

1.
you.   Bit - ter - you. _____

2.

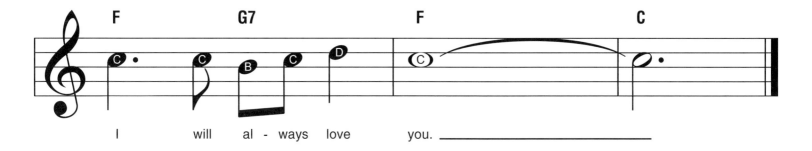

I will al - ways love you. _____

I Wouldn't Have Missed It
for the World

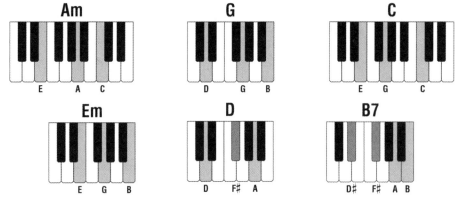

Words and Music by Kye Fleming,
Dennis Morgan and Charles Quillen

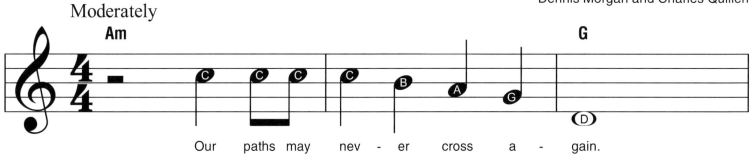

Our paths may nev - er cross a - gain.

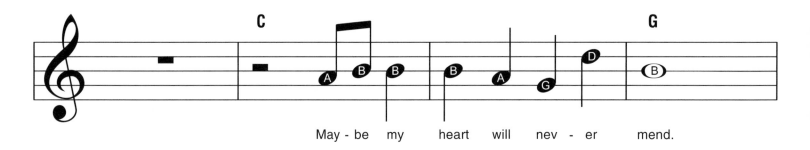

May - be my heart will nev - er mend.

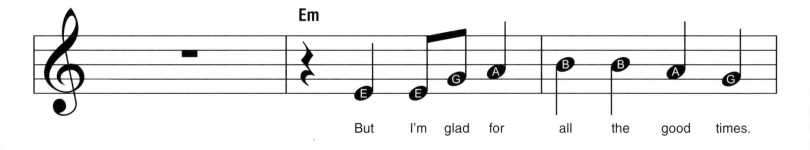

But I'm glad for all the good times.

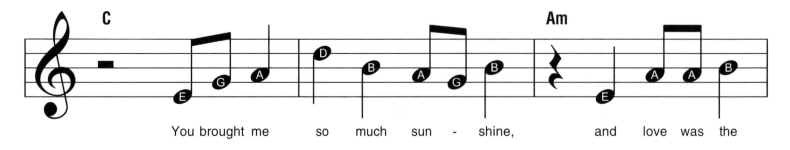

You brought me so much sun - shine, and love was the

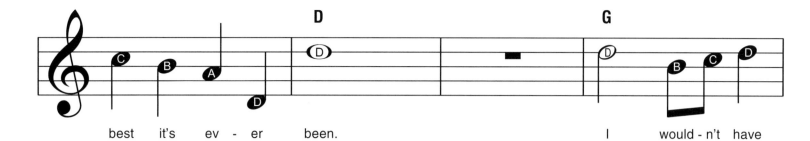

best it's ev - er been. I would - n't have

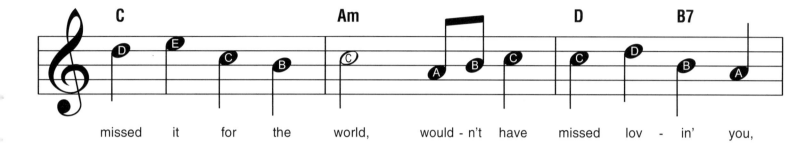

missed it for the world, would - n't have missed lov - in' you,

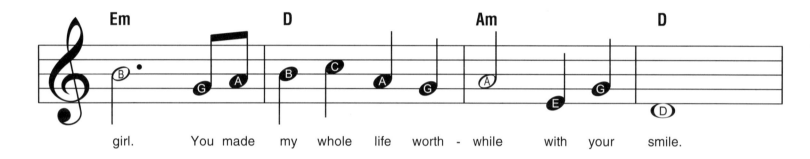

girl. You made my whole life worth - while with your smile.

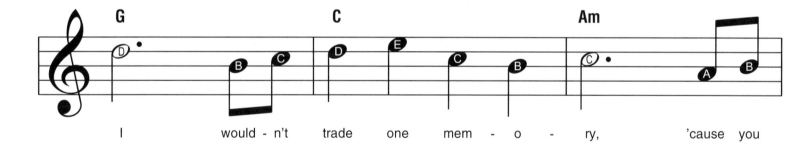

I would - n't trade one mem - o - ry, 'cause you

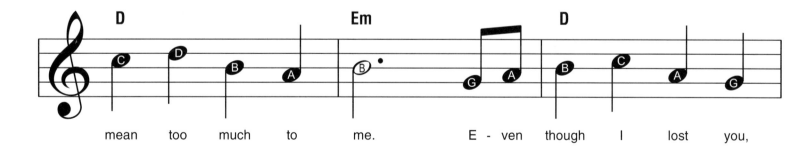

mean too much to me. E - ven though I lost you,

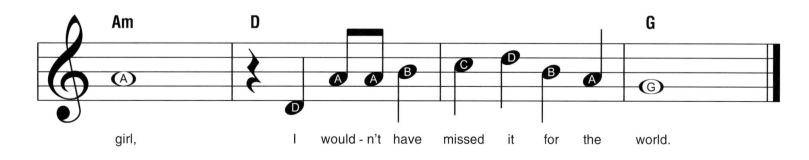

girl, I would - n't have missed it for the world.

Islands in the Stream

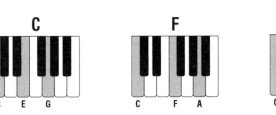
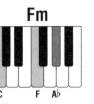
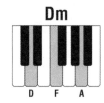

Words and Music by Barry Gibb,
Robin Gibb and Maurice Gibb

It Wasn't God Who Made Honky Tonk Angels

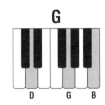

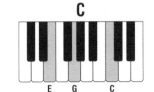

Words and Music by
J.D. Miller

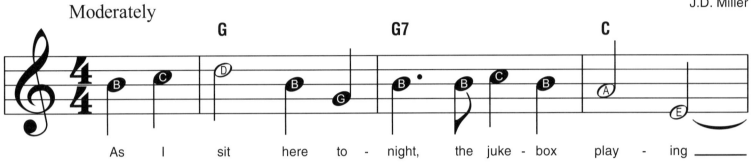

As I sit here to-night, the juke-box play-ing _____

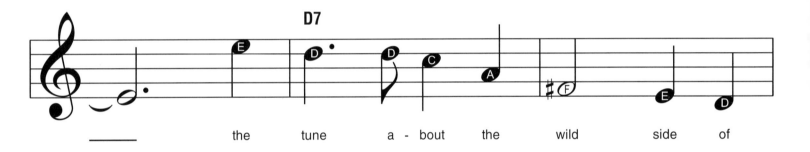

_____ the tune a-bout the wild side of

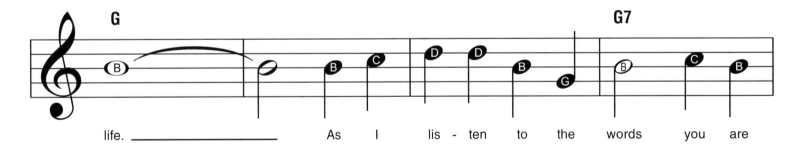

life. _____ As I lis-ten to the words you are

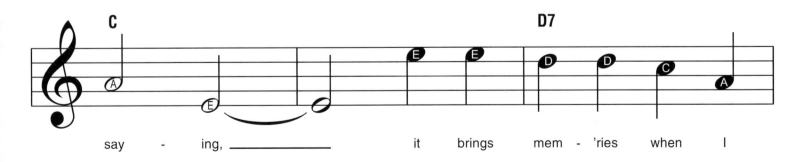

say-ing, _____ it brings mem-'ries when I

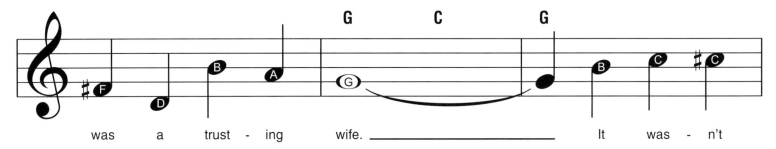

was a trust - ing wife. _____ It was - n't

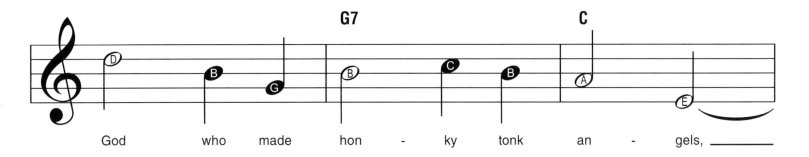

God who made hon - ky tonk an - gels, _____

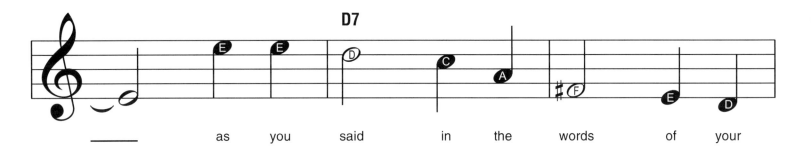

_____ as you said in the words of your

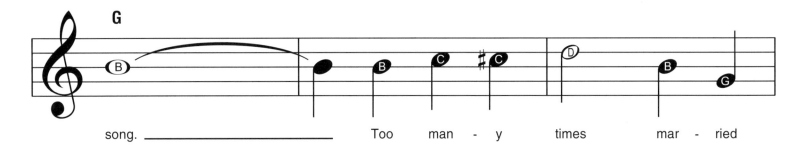

song. _____ Too man - y times mar - ried

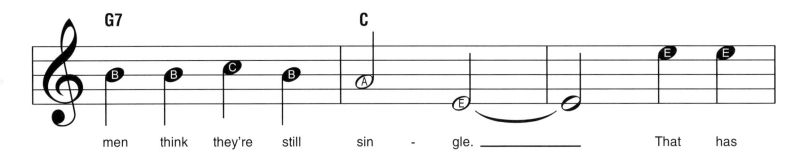

men think they're still sin - gle. _____ That has

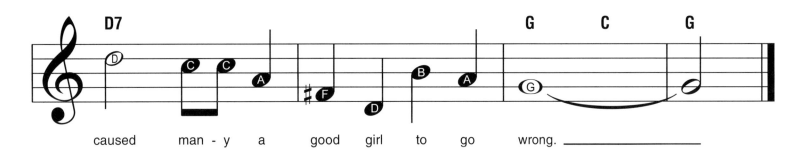

caused man - y a good girl to go wrong. _____

Jambalaya
(On the Bayou)

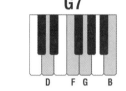

Words and Music by
Hank Williams

69

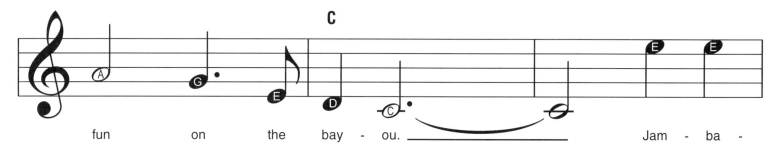

fun on the bay - ou. _____ Jam - ba -

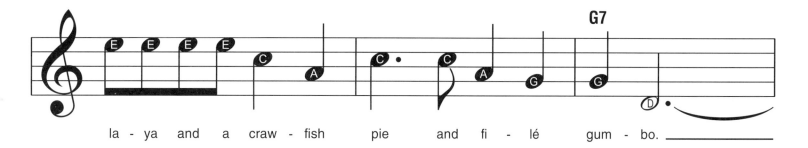

la - ya and a craw - fish pie and fi - lé gum - bo. _____

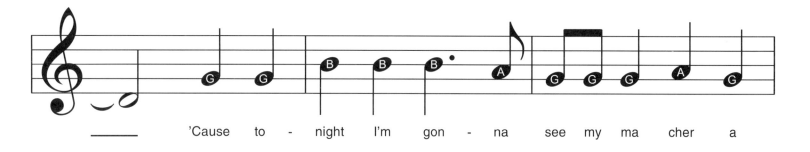

_____ 'Cause to - night I'm gon - na see my ma cher a

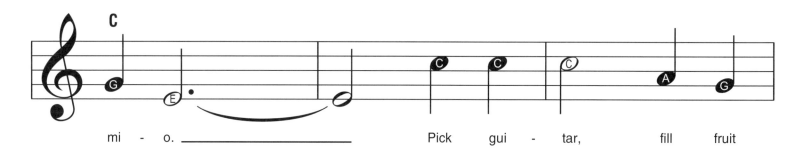

mi - o. _____ Pick gui - tar, fill fruit

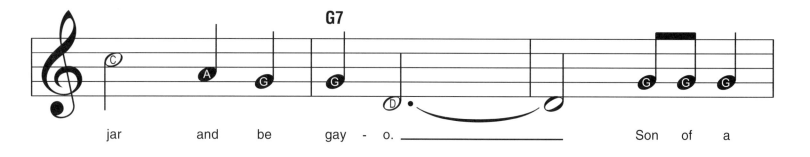

jar and be gay - o. _____ Son of a

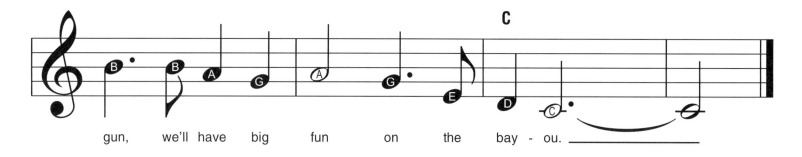

gun, we'll have big fun on the bay - ou. _____

King of the Road

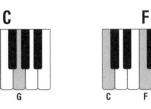
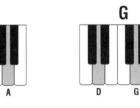

Words and Music by
Roger Miller

Moderate Shuffle

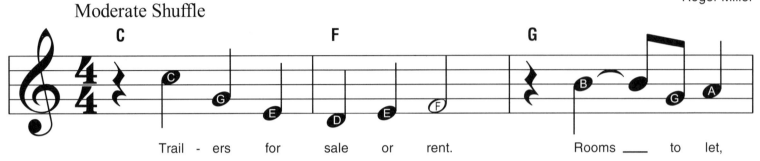

Trail - ers for sale or rent. Rooms ___ to let,

fif - ty cents. No phone, no pool, no pets.

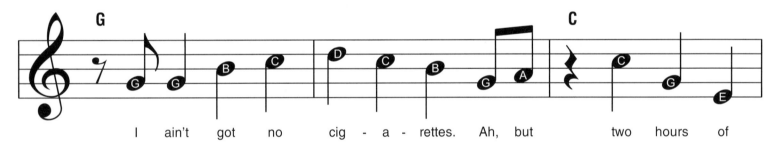

I ain't got no cig - a - rettes. Ah, but two hours of

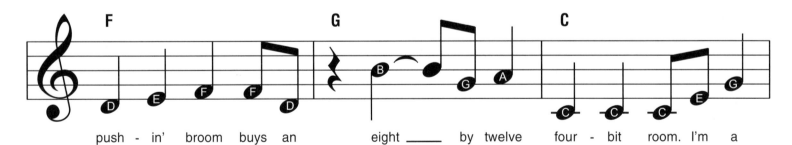

push - in' broom buys an eight ___ by twelve four - bit room. I'm a

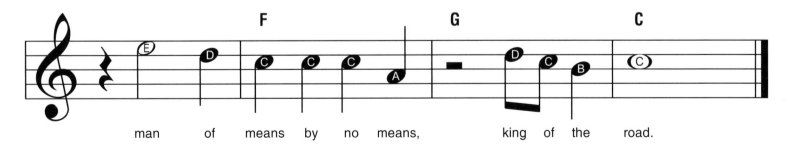

man of means by no means, king of the road.

Luckenbach, Texas
(Back to the Basics of Love)

Words and Music by Bobby Emmons
and Chips Moman

Kiss an Angel Good Mornin'

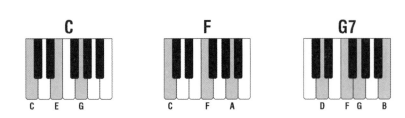

Words and Music by
Ben Peters

Moderate Shuffle

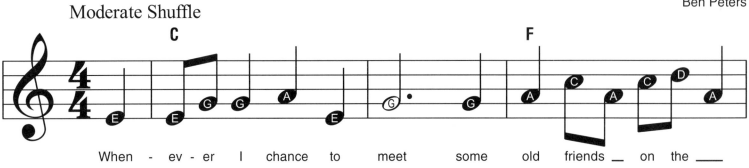

When - ev - er I chance to meet some old friends __ on the __

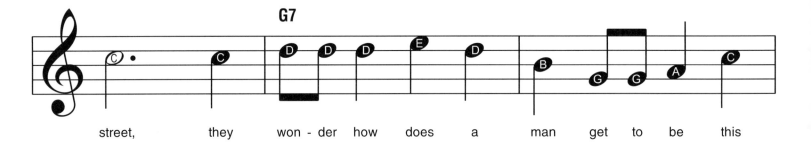

street, they won - der how does a man get to be this

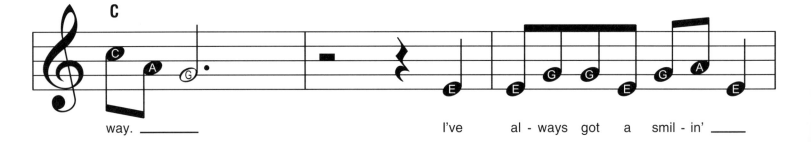

way. _____ I've al - ways got a smil - in' _____

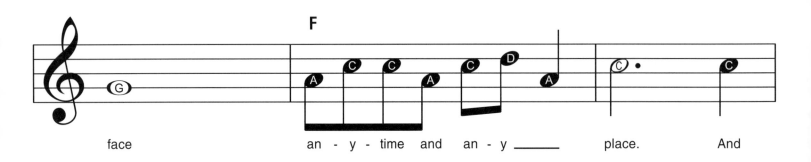

face an - y - time and an - y _____ place. And

73

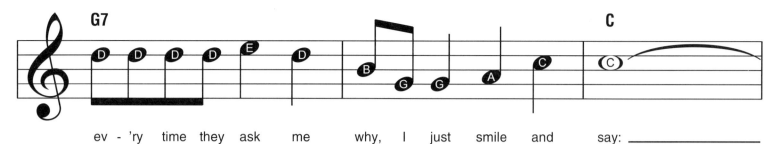

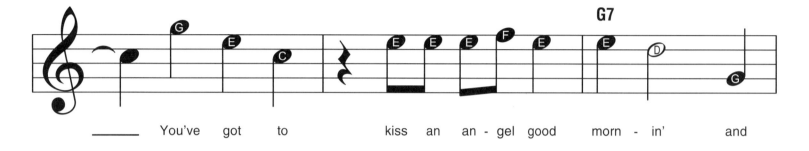

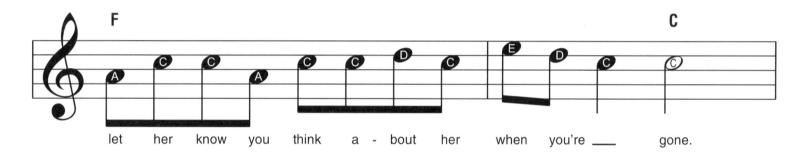

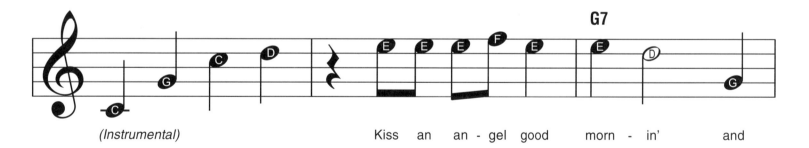

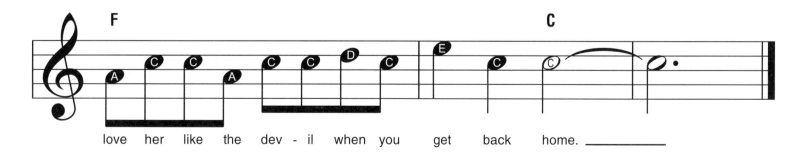

Little Green Apples

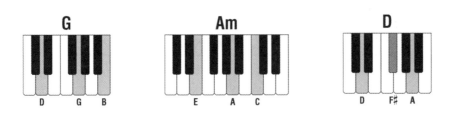

Words and Music by
Bobby Russell

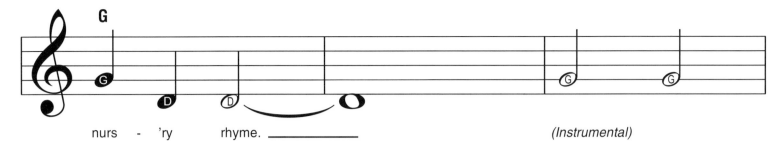

nurs - 'ry   rhyme. _____   *(Instrumental)*

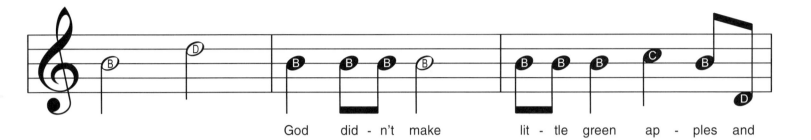

God   did - n't   make   lit - tle   green   ap - ples   and

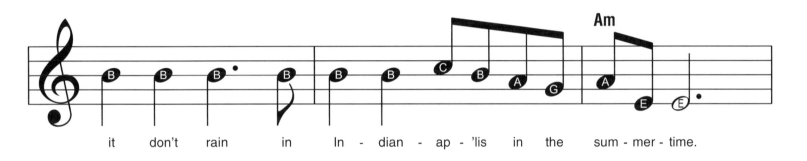

it   don't   rain   in   In - dian - ap - 'lis   in   the   sum - mer - time.

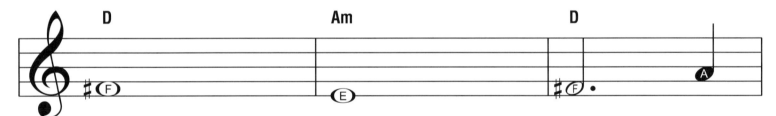

(Instrumental)   And

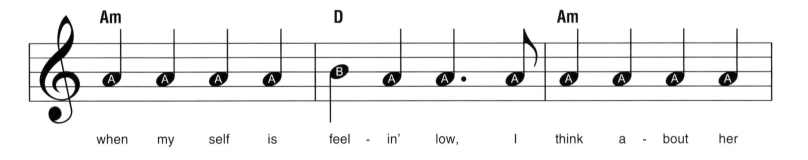

when   my   self   is   feel - in'   low,   I   think   a - bout   her

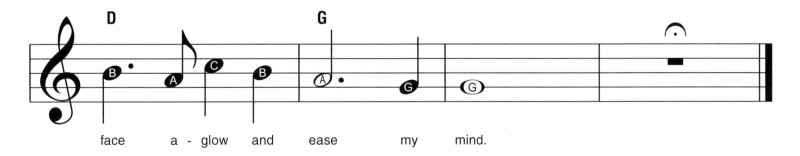

face   a - glow   and   ease   my   mind.

Love Without End, Amen

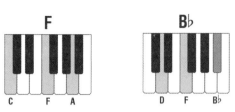
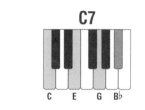

Words and Music by
Aaron G. Barker

Moderately fast

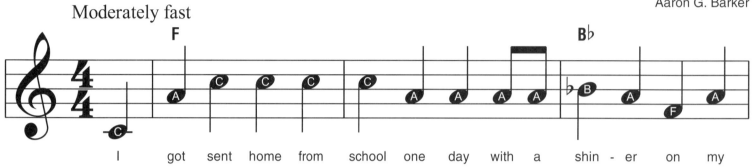

I got sent home from school one day with a shin - er on my

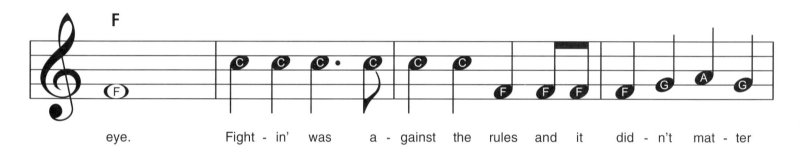

eye. Fight - in' was a - gainst the rules and it did - n't mat - ter

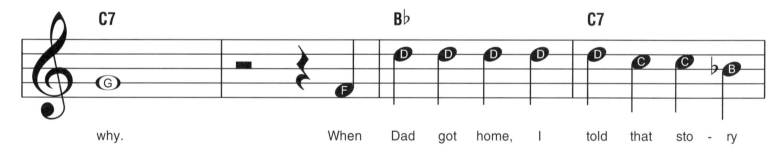

why. When Dad got home, I told that sto - ry

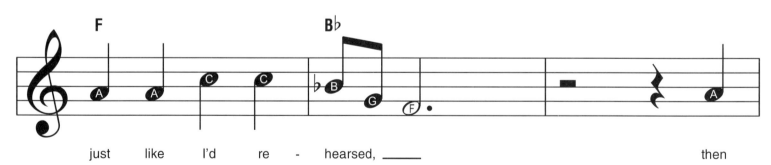

just like I'd re - hearsed, ____ then

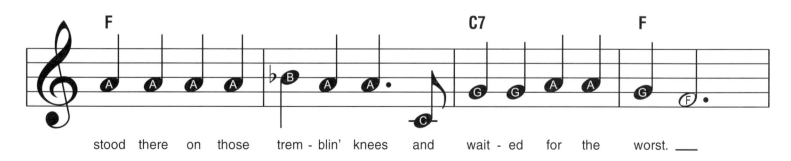

stood there on those trem - blin' knees and wait - ed for the worst. ____

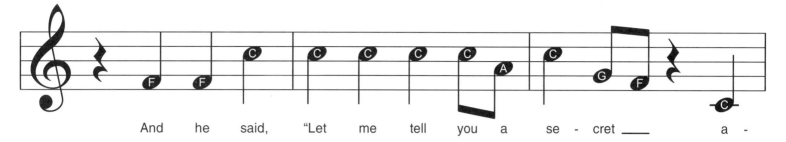

And he said, "Let me tell you a se- cret ____ a-

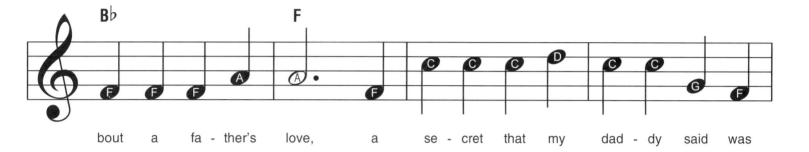

bout a fa - ther's love, a se- cret that my dad - dy said was

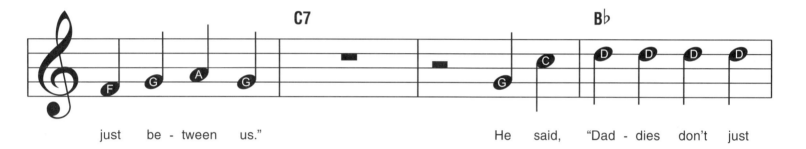

just be - tween us." He said, "Dad - dies don't just

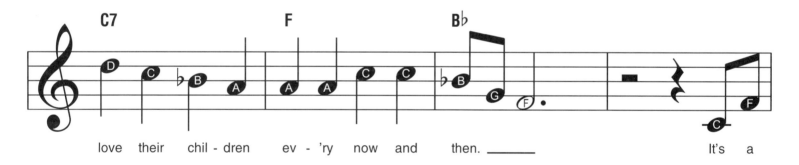

love their chil - dren ev - 'ry now and then. _____ It's a

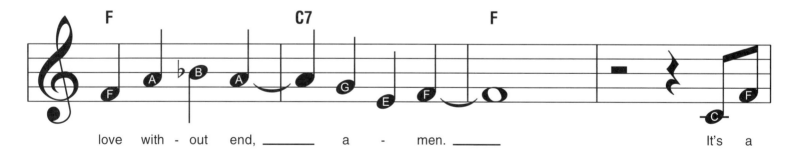

love with - out end, _____ a - men. _____ It's a

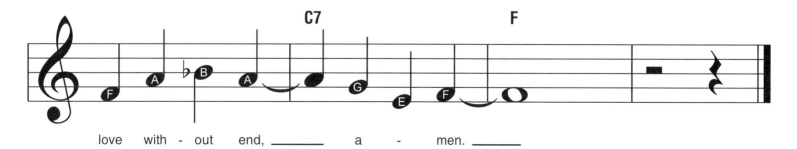

love with - out end, _____ a - men. _____

Make the World Go Away

Words and Music by
Hank Cochran

Release Me

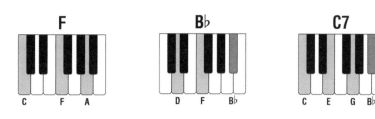

Words and Music by Robert Yount,
Eddie Miller and Dub Williams

Mammas Don't Let Your Babies Grow Up to Be Cowboys

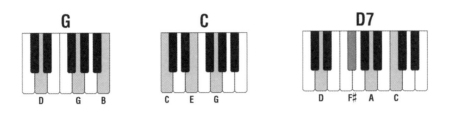

Words and Music by Ed Bruce
and Patsy Bruce

Moderately fast

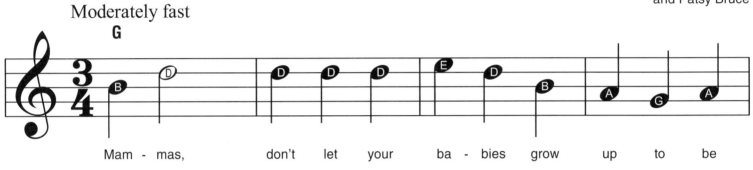

Mam - mas, don't let your ba - bies grow up to be

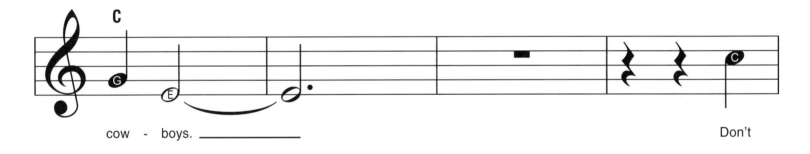

cow - boys. _____ Don't

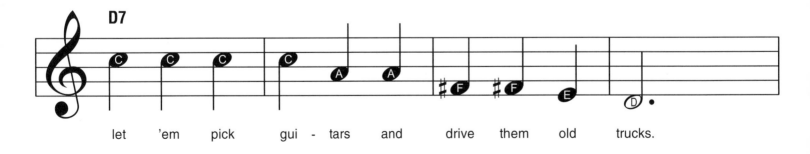

let 'em pick gui - tars and drive them old trucks.

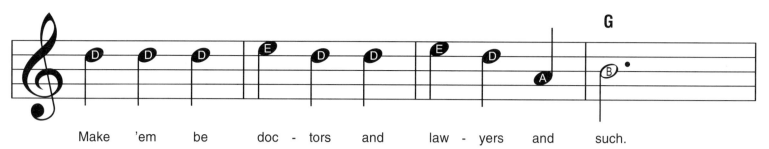

Make 'em be doc - tors and law - yers and such.

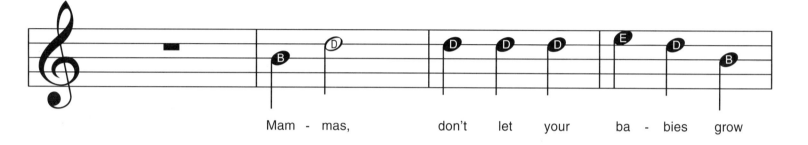

Mam - mas, don't let your ba - bies grow

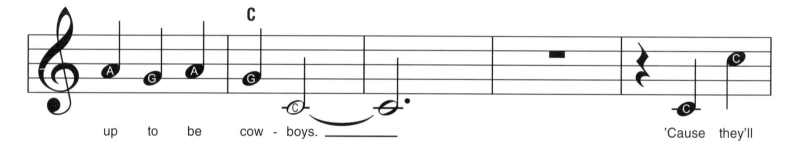

up to be cow - boys. _____ 'Cause they'll

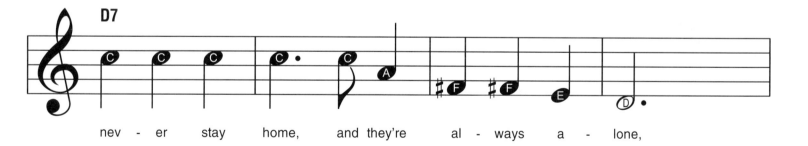

nev - er stay home, and they're al - ways a - lone,

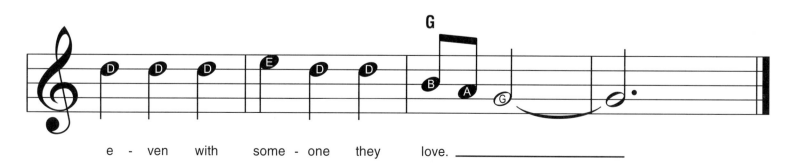

e - ven with some - one they love. _____

My Heroes Have Always Been Cowboys

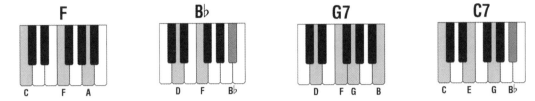

Words and Music by
Sharon Vaughn

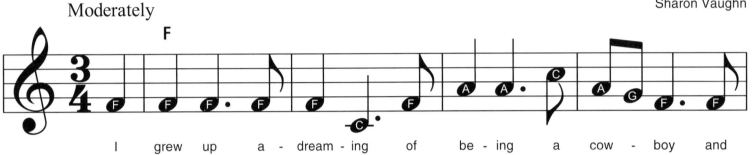

Moderately

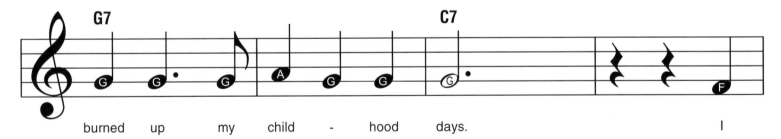

I grew up a-dream-ing of be-ing a cow-boy and

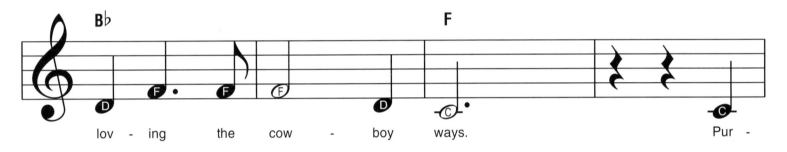

lov-ing the cow-boy ways. Pur-

su-ing the life of my high-rid-in' he-roes, ___ I

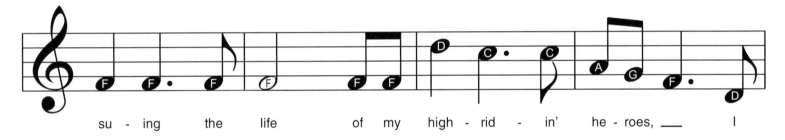

burned up my child-hood days. I

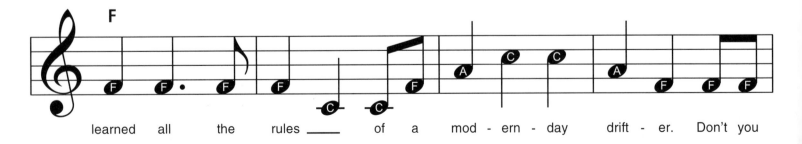

learned all the rules ___ of a mod-ern-day drift-er. Don't you

Oh, Lonesome Me

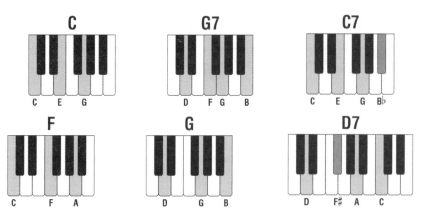

Words and Music by
Don Gibson

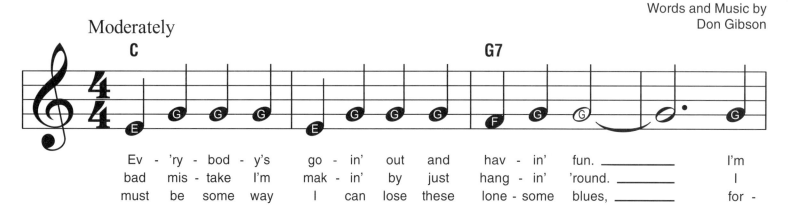

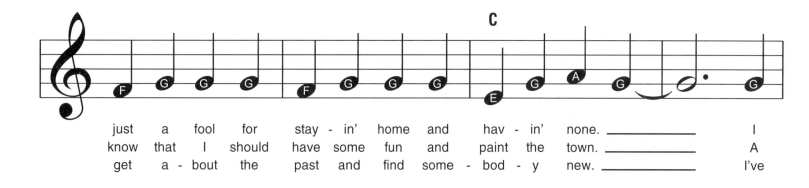

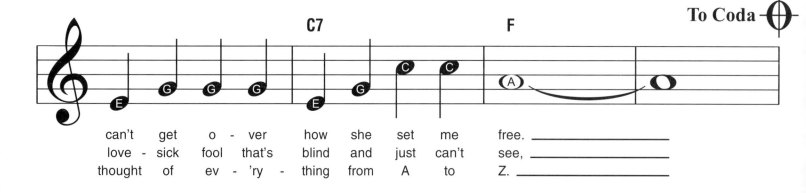

On the Road Again

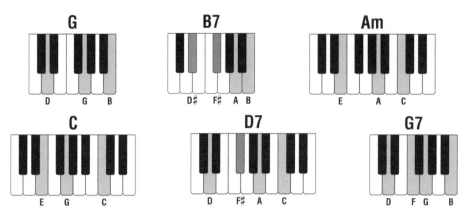

Words and Music by
Willie Nelson

Our Song

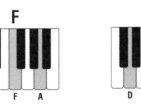
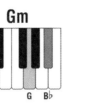
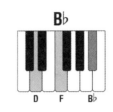
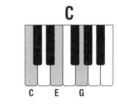

Words and Music by
Taylor Swift

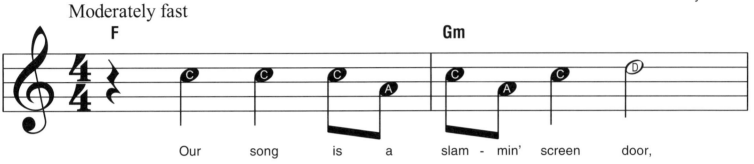

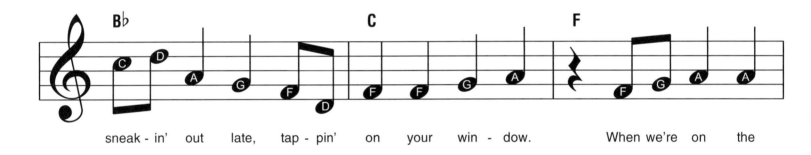

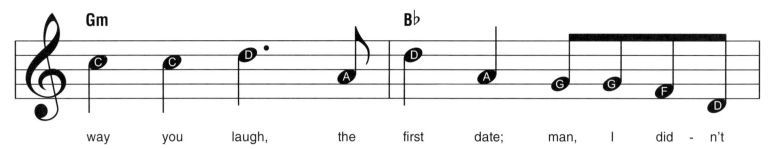

way   you   laugh,   the   first   date;   man,   I   did - n't

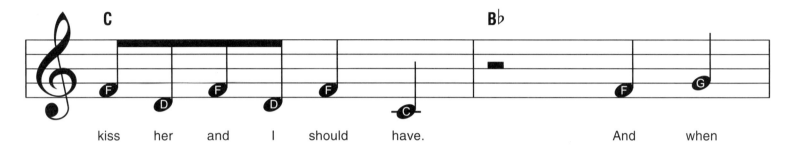

kiss   her   and   I   should   have.   And   when

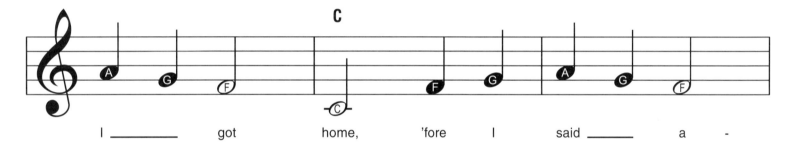

I _____ got   home,   'fore   I   said _____ a -

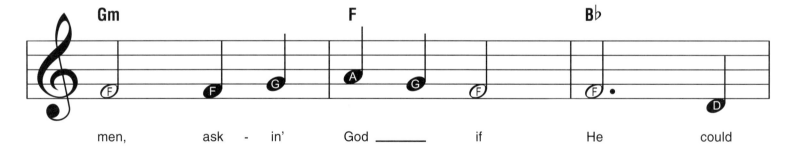

men,   ask - in'   God _____ if   He   could

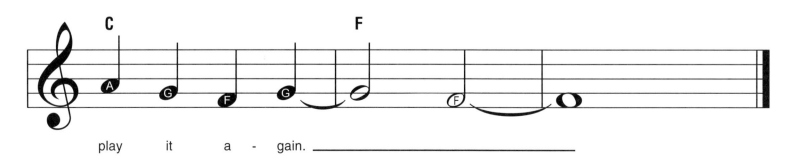

play   it   a - gain. _____

Rhinestone Cowboy

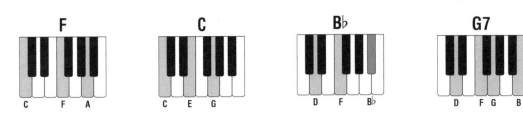

Words and Music by
Larry Weiss

Rocky Top

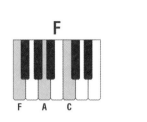
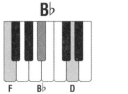
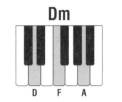
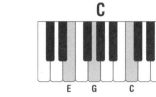
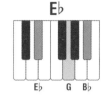

Words and Music by Boudleaux Bryant
and Felice Bryant

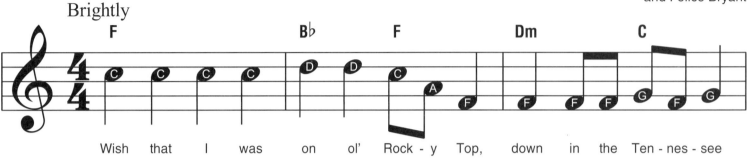

Wish that I was on ol' Rock - y Top, down in the Ten - nes - see

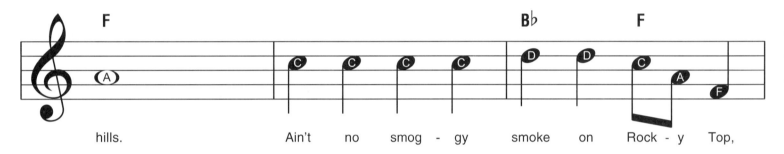

hills. Ain't no smog - gy smoke on Rock - y Top,

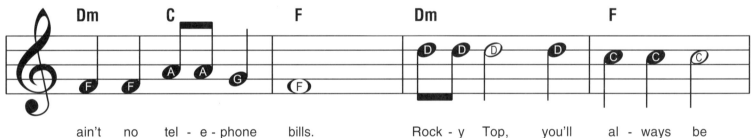

ain't no tel - e - phone bills. Rock - y Top, you'll al - ways be

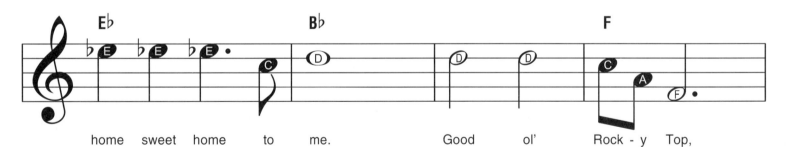

home sweet home to me. Good ol' Rock - y Top,

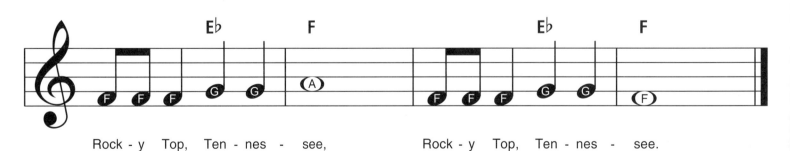

Rock - y Top, Ten - nes - see, Rock - y Top, Ten - nes - see.

(I Never Promised You A)
Rose Garden

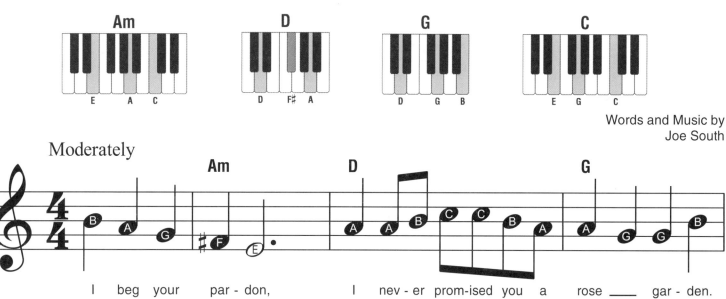

Words and Music by
Joe South

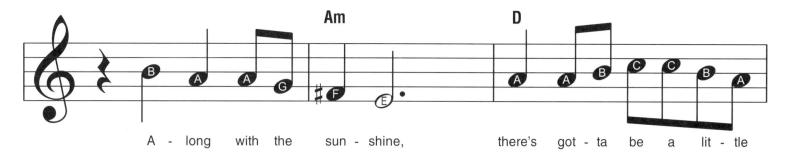

I beg your par - don,   I nev - er prom-ised you a   rose ____ gar - den.

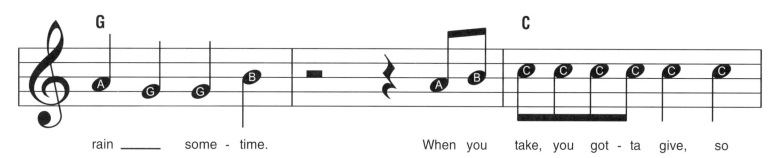

A - long   with the   sun - shine,   there's got - ta be a   lit - tle

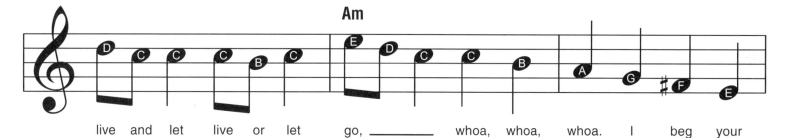

rain ____   some - time.   When you   take, you got - ta give, so

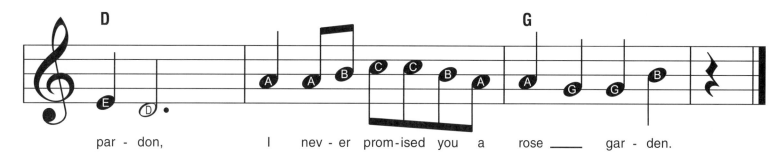

live and let   live or let   go, ____   whoa,   whoa,   whoa.   I   beg   your

par - don,   I nev - er prom-ised you a   rose ____ gar - den.

Ruby, Don't Take Your Love to Town

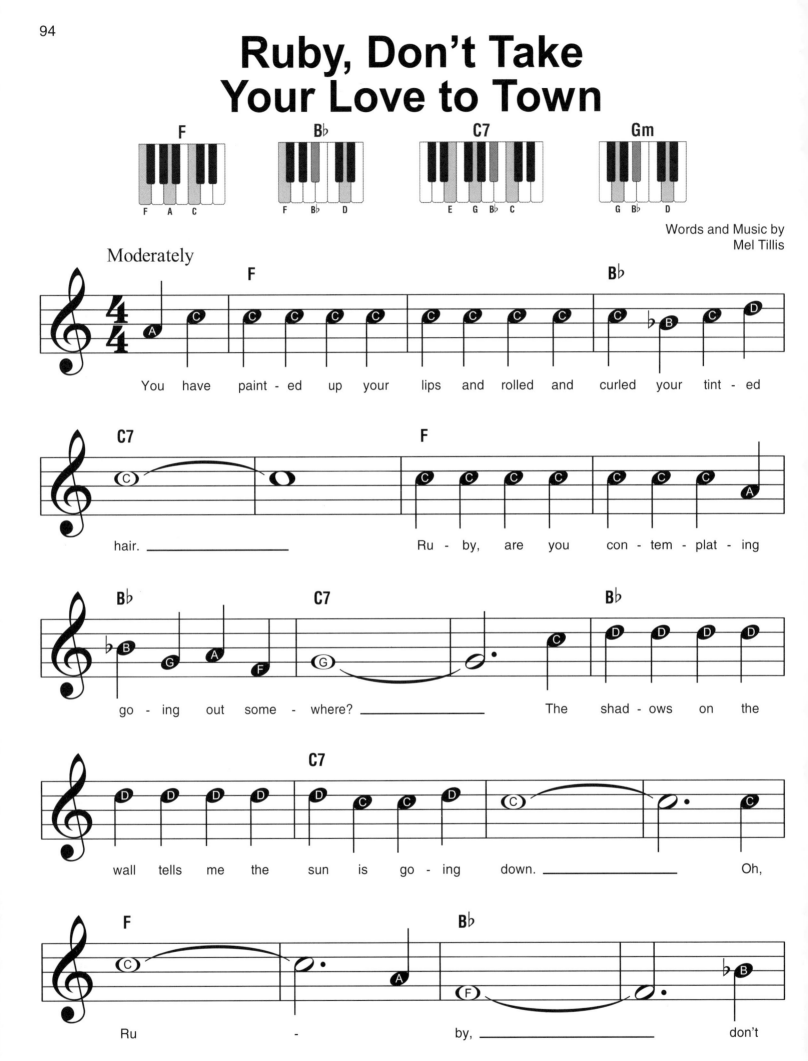

Words and Music by
Mel Tillis

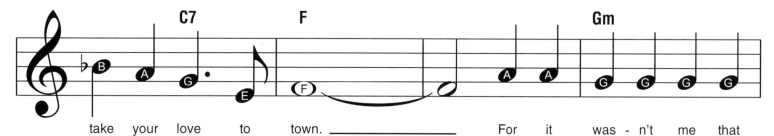

take your love to town. _____ For it was-n't me that

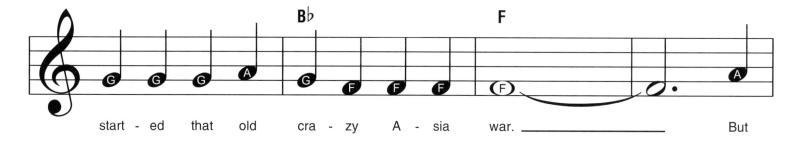

start - ed that old cra - zy A - sia war. _____ But

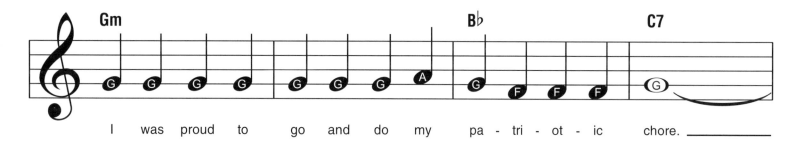

I was proud to go and do my pa - tri - ot - ic chore. _____

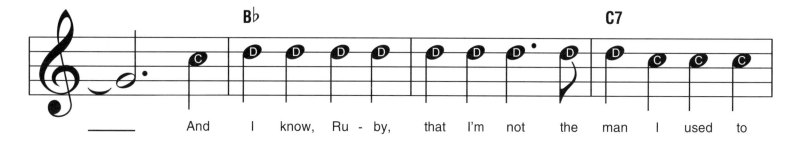

_____ And I know, Ru - by, that I'm not the man I used to

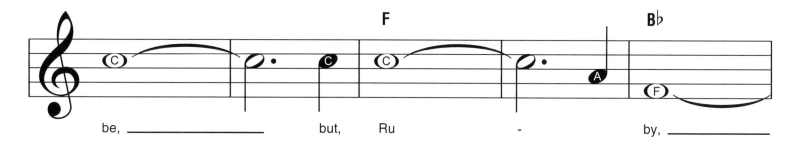

be, _____ but, Ru - by, _____

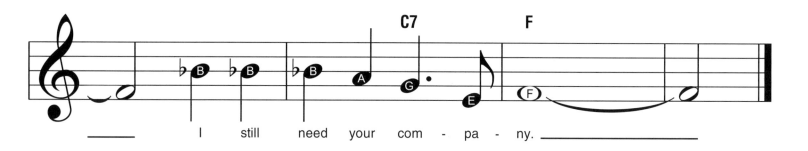

_____ I still need your com - pa - ny. _____

Send Me the Pillow You Dream On

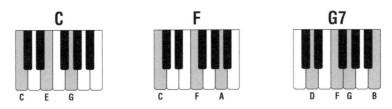

Words and Music by
Hank Locklin

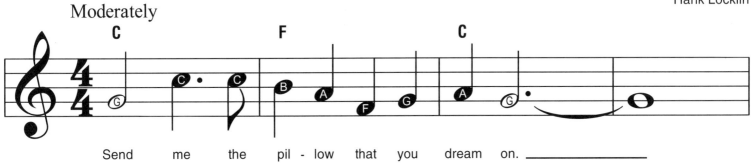

Send me the pil - low that you dream on. _____

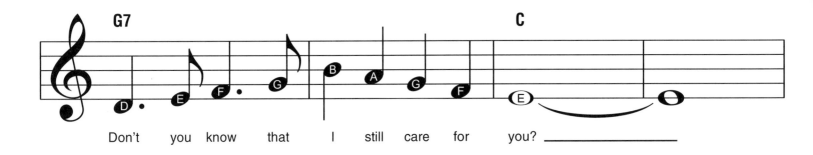

Don't you know that I still care for you? _____

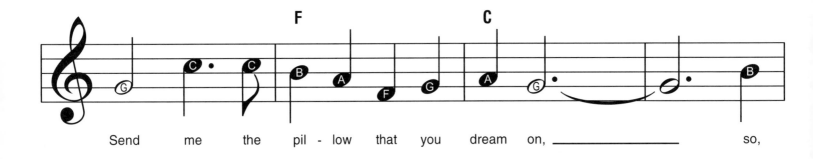

Send me the pil - low that you dream on, _____ so,

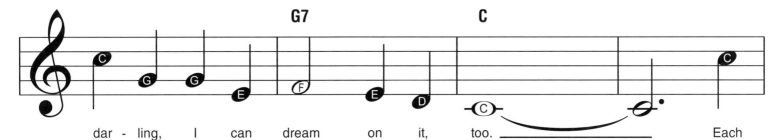

dar - ling, I can dream on it, too. _____ Each

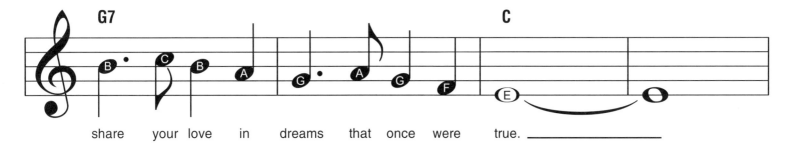

night while I'm sleep - ing, oh, so lone - ly, _____ I'll

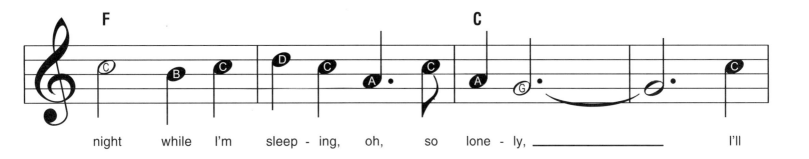

share your love in dreams that once were true. _____

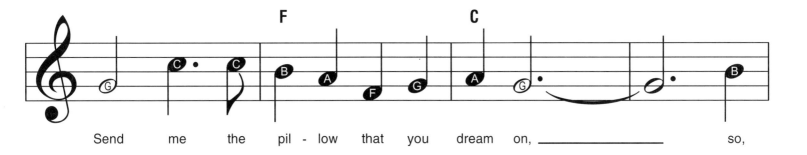

Send me the pil - low that you dream on, _____ so,

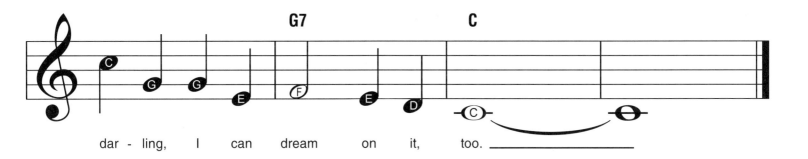

dar - ling, I can dream on it, too. _____

She Believes in Me

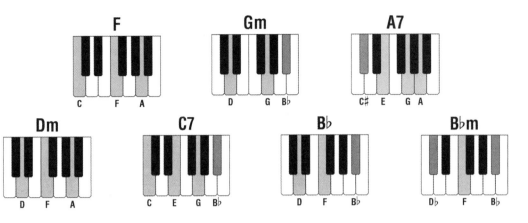

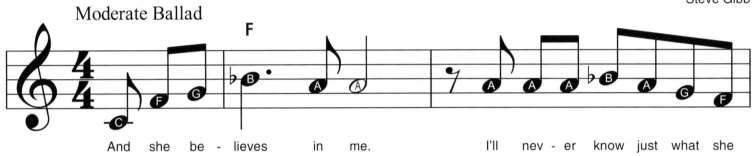

Words and Music by
Steve Gibb

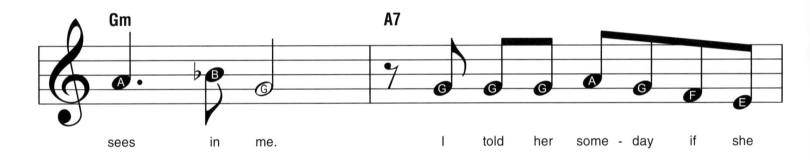

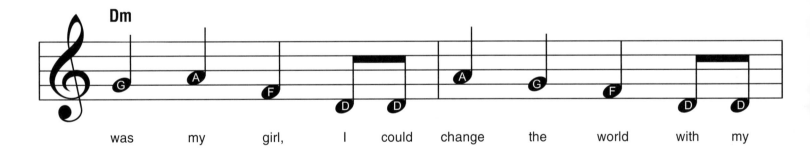

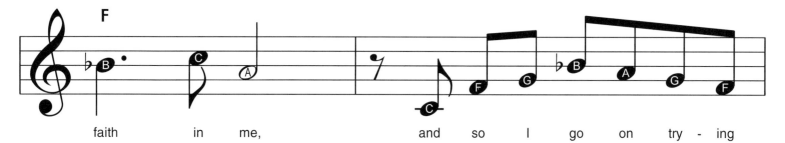

faith in me, and so I go on try - ing

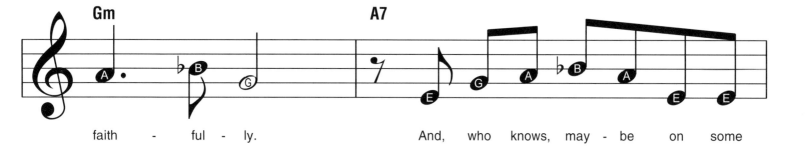

faith - ful - ly. And, who knows, may - be on some

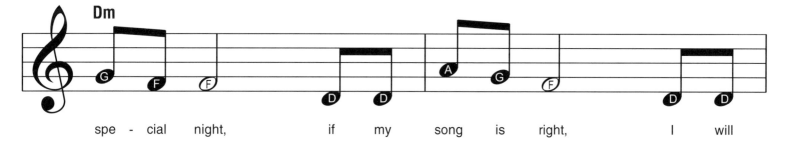

spe - cial night, if my song is right, I will

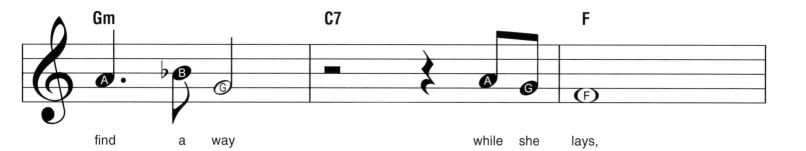

find a way while she lays,

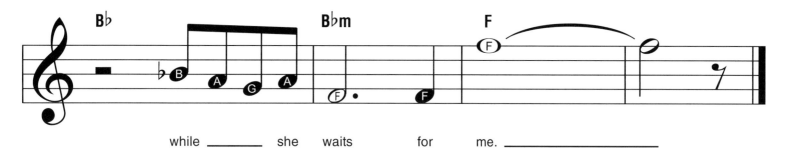

while _____ she waits for me. _____

Southern Nights

Words and Music by
Allen Toussaint

Take These Chains from My Heart

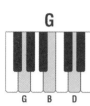
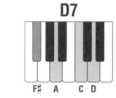
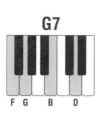
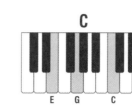
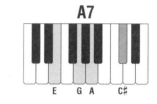

Words and Music by Fred Rose
and Hy Heath

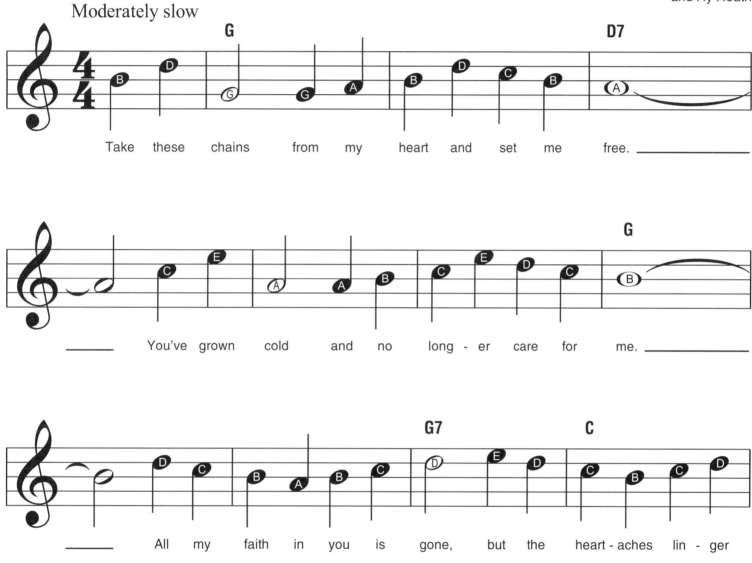

Take these chains from my heart and set me free. ____

____ You've grown cold and no long-er care for me. ____

____ All my faith in you is gone, but the heart-aches lin-ger

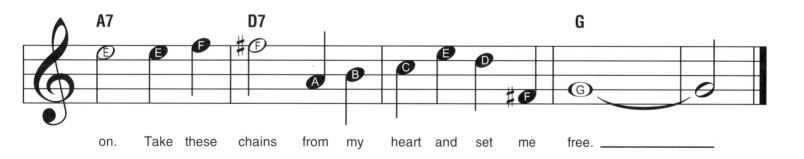

on. Take these chains from my heart and set me free. ____

Stand By Your Man

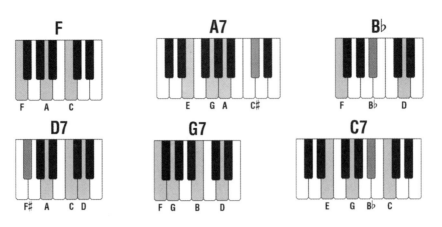

Words and Music by Tammy Wynette
and Billy Sherrill

Moderate Shuffle

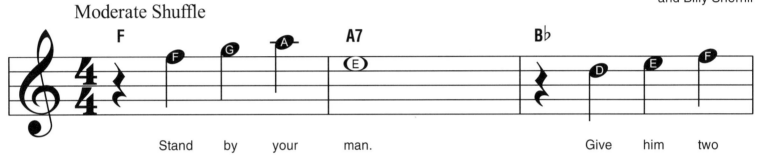

Stand by your man. Give him two

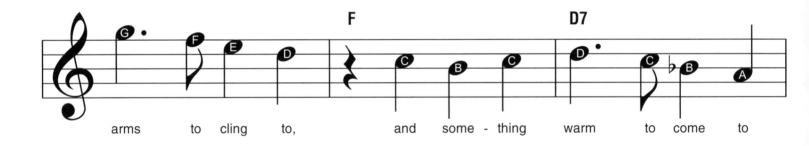

arms to cling to, and some-thing warm to come to

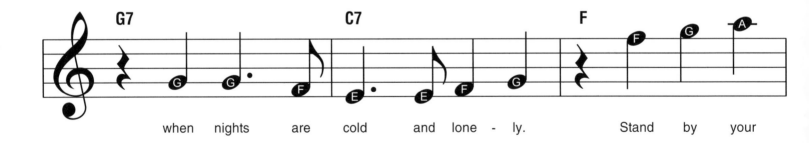

when nights are cold and lone-ly. Stand by your

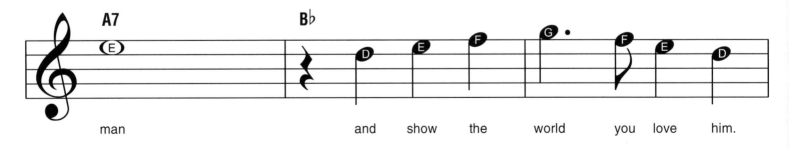

man and show the world you love him.

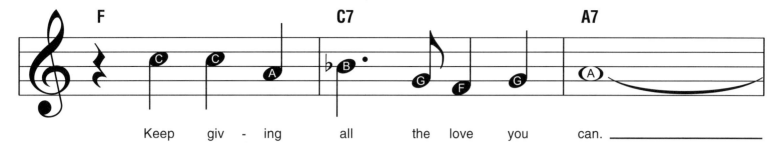

Keep giv - ing all the love you can. _____

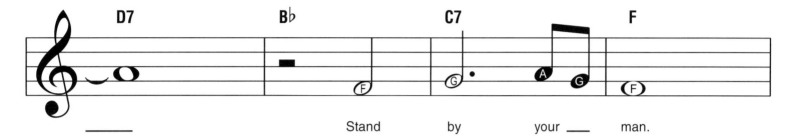

_____ Stand by your ___ man.

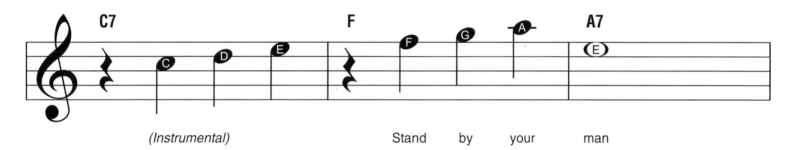

(Instrumental) Stand by your man

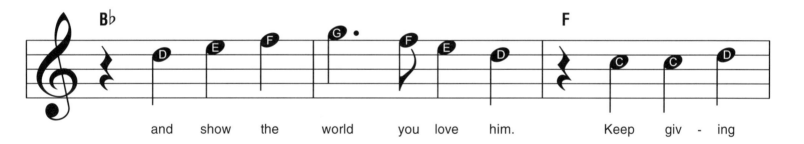

and show the world you love him. Keep giv - ing

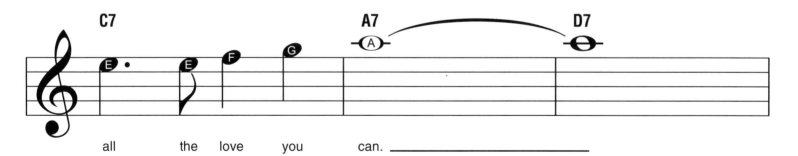

all the love you can. _____

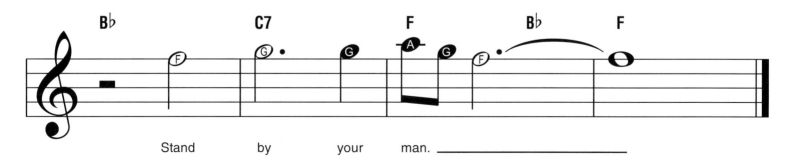

Stand by your man. _____

Through the Years

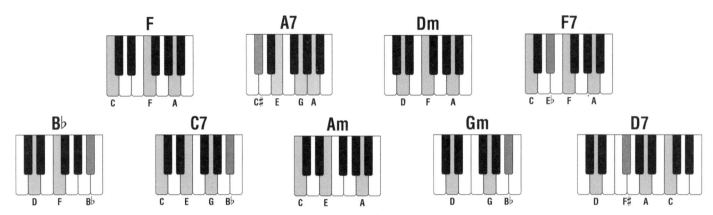

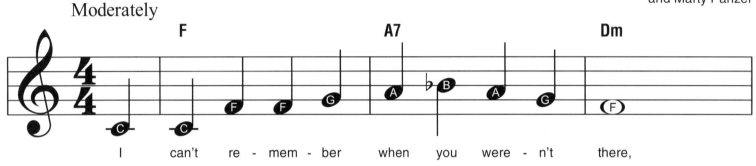

Words and Music by Steve Dorff
and Marty Panzer

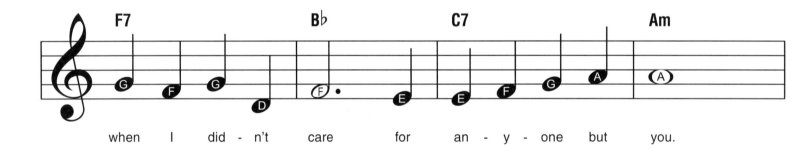

I can't re - mem - ber when you were - n't there,

when I did - n't care for an - y - one but you.

I swear _____ we've been through ev - 'ry - thing there

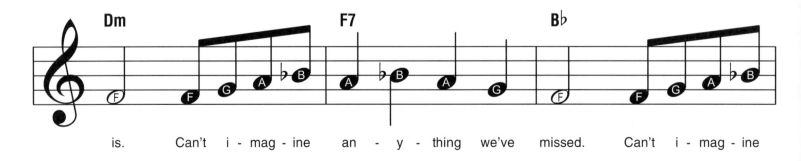

is. Can't i - mag - ine an - y - thing we've missed. Can't i - mag - ine

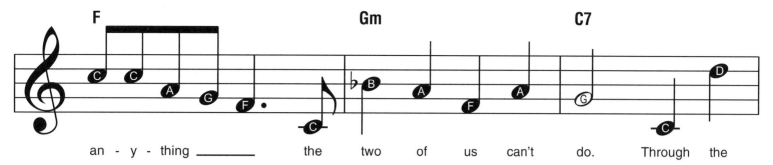

an - y - thing _____ the two of us can't do. Through the

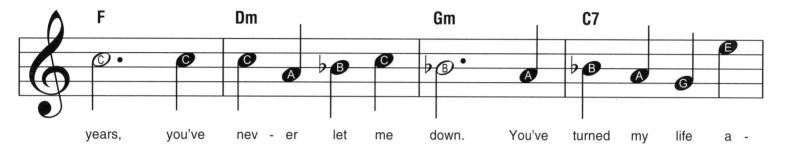

years, you've nev - er let me down. You've turned my life a -

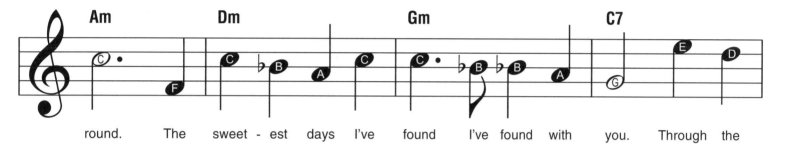

round. The sweet - est days I've found I've found with you. Through the

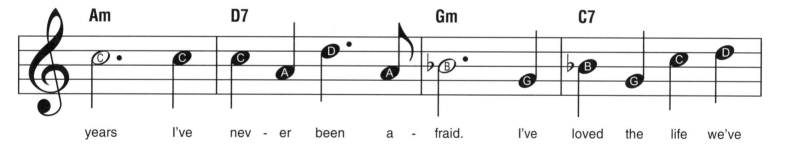

years I've nev - er been a - fraid. I've loved the life we've

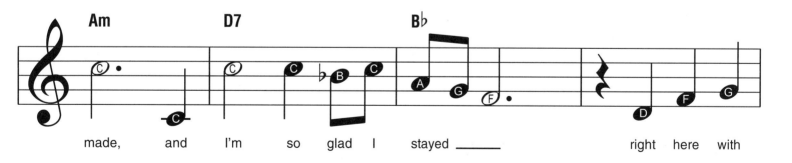

made, and I'm so glad I stayed _____ right here with

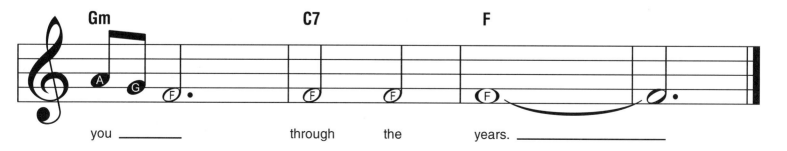

you _____ through the years. _____

Wagon Wheel

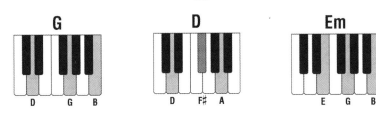

Words and Music by Bob Dylan
and Ketch Secor

Moderate Country Shuffle

Head-in' down south to the land of the pines, ___ I'm thumb-in' my way out of

North Car-o-line. Star-in' up the road and pray to God I see

head-lights. I made it down the coast in

sev-en-teen hours. Pick-in' me a bou-quet of dog-wood flow'rs. And I'm a-

hop-in' for Ra-leigh, I can see my ba-by to-night. ___

What's Forever For

Words and Music by
Rafe Van Hoy

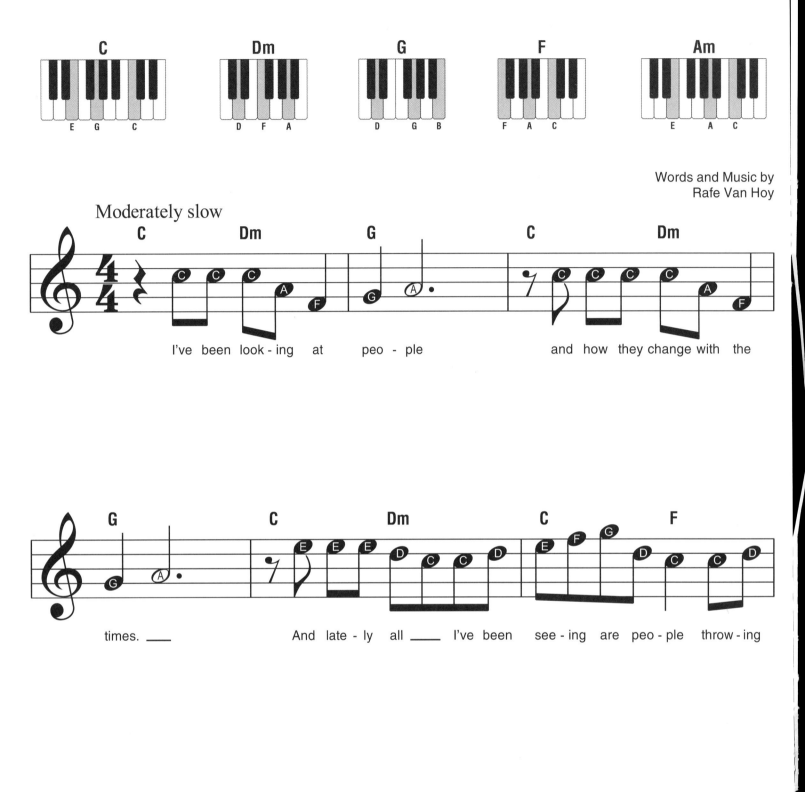

I've been look-ing at peo-ple and how they change with the times. ___ And late-ly all ___ I've been see-ing are peo-ple throw-ing

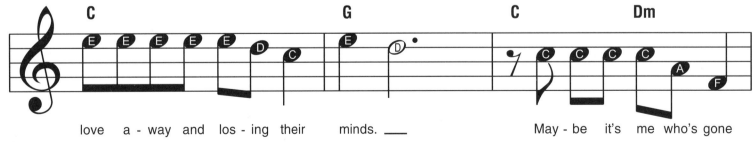

love a-way and los-ing their minds. ___ May-be it's me who's gone

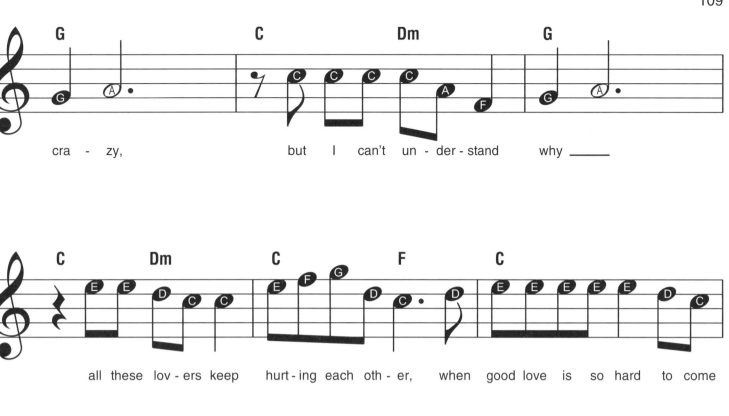

cra - zy,   but   I   can't   un - der - stand   why _____

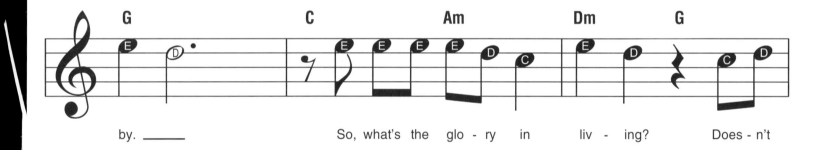

all   these   lov - ers   keep   hurt - ing   each   oth - er,   when   good   love   is   so   hard   to   come

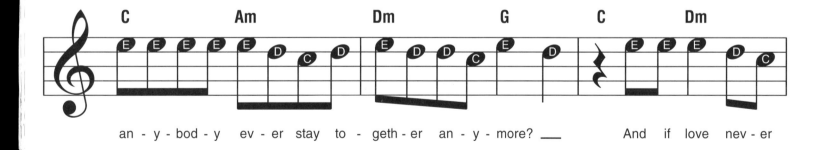

by. _____   So,   what's   the   glo - ry   in   liv - ing?   Does - n't

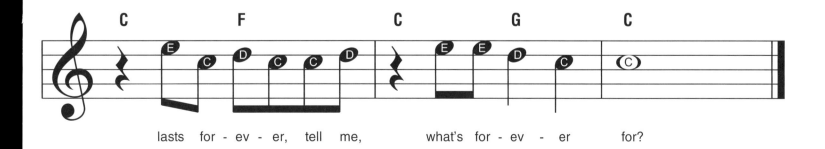

an - y - bod - y   ev - er   stay   to - geth - er   an - y - more? ___   And   if   love   nev - er

lasts   for - ev - er,   tell   me,   what's   for - ev - er   for?

You're Still the One

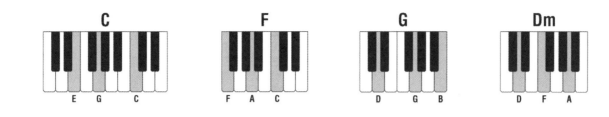

Words and Music by Shania Twain
and R.J. Lange

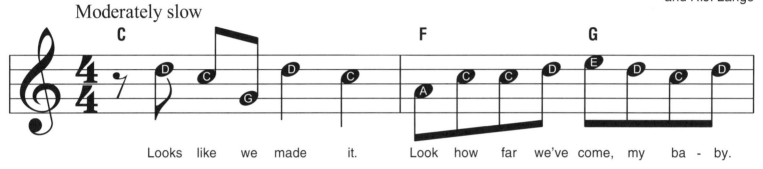

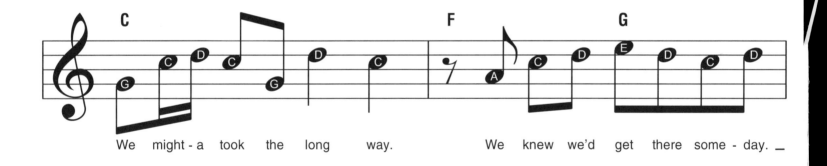

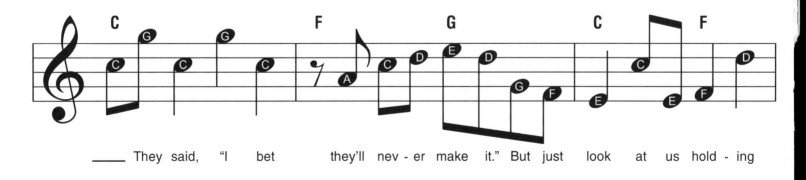

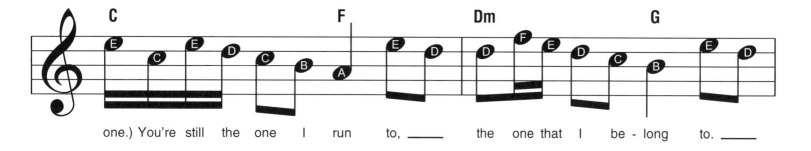

on. We're still to - geth - er, still go - ing strong. (You're still the

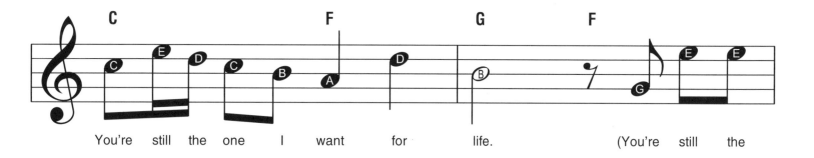

one.) You're still the one I run to, _____ the one that I be - long to. _____

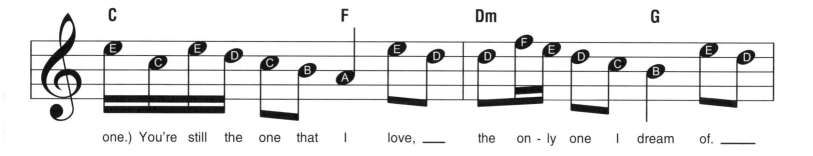

You're still the one I want for life. (You're still the

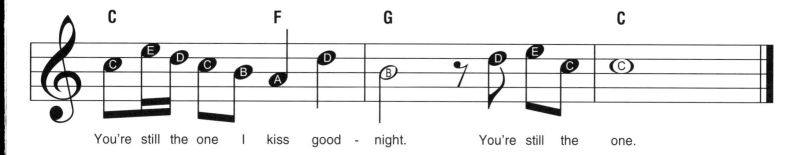

one.) You're still the one that I love, __ the on - ly one I dream of. _____

You're still the one I kiss good - night. You're still the one.

Wichita Lineman

Words and Music by
Jimmy Webb